The Journey of a Lifetime 2

Connecting
Developing Closeness on the Journey of a Lifetime

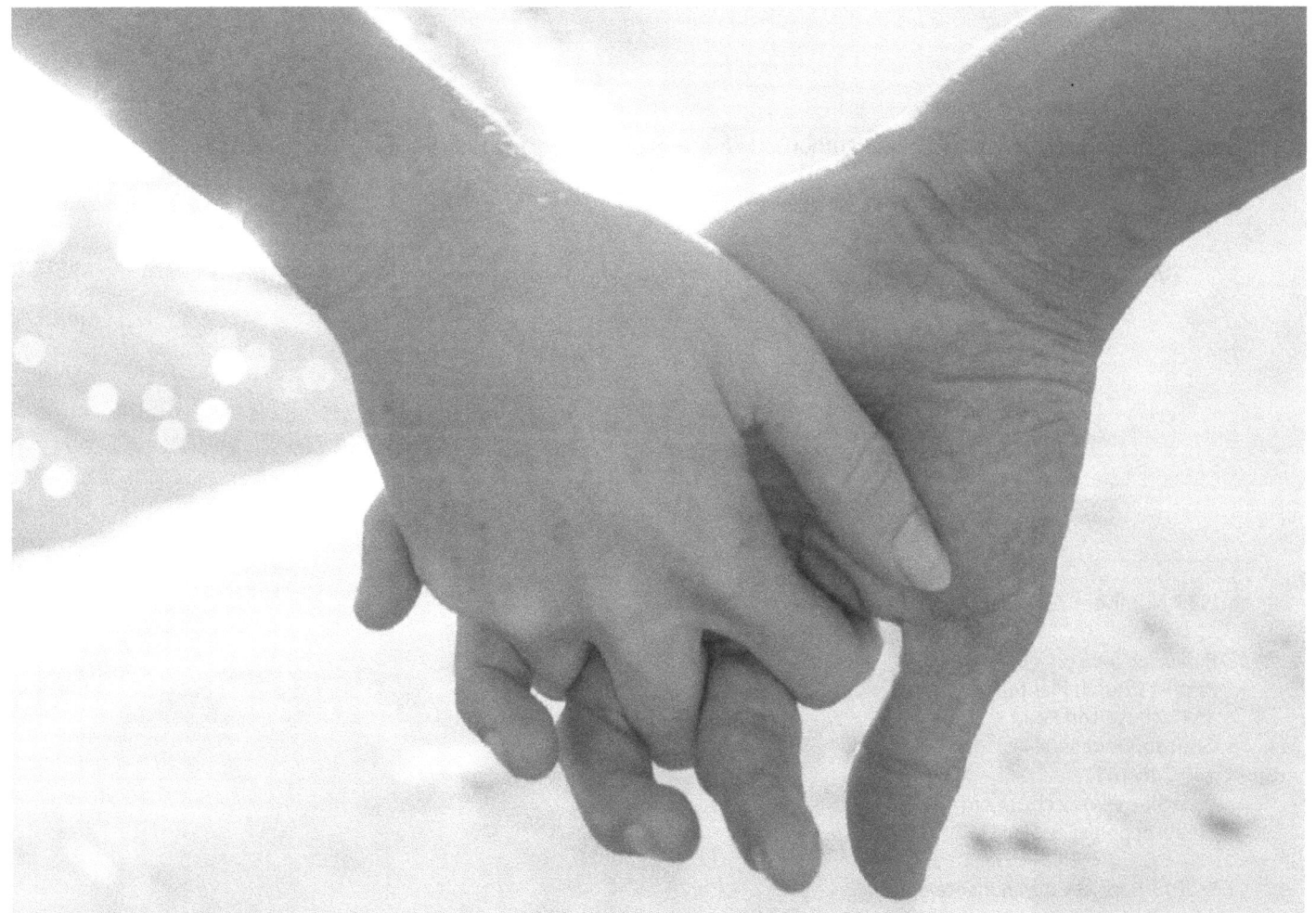

Leader's Edition

Dr. Michael J. Peck

All Scripture quotations are from the Authorized King James Version of the Holy Bible.

ISBN Number 978-1-936285-03-7

Published by:
Baptist Church Planters
36830 Royalton Road
Grafton, Ohio 44044
440-748-1677
Web Site: www.bcpusa.org
Email: bcp@bcpusa.org

© 2011 Baptist Church Planters

All rights reserved. No part of this publication may be reproduced, stored in a retrieval system, or transmitted in any form or by any means, electronic, mechanical, photocopying, recording, or otherwise, without prior written permission of the publisher.

Cover design by an idea - anideaweb.com

To our married children and their spouses

Your Mother and I thank the Lord for you.
We pray that you will always know the joy of
Connecting—Developing Closeness
on the Journey of a Lifetime.

Acknowledgements

A very special thank you goes to my dear wife, Karen. She is my best friend. Her faithful walk with the Lord, her love for me, and her commitment to our marriage makes writing a marriage series not only possible, but a joy.

To my friends, Robert Bowker and Lawrence Montgomery, thank you for the hours you invested on the manuscript. The Lord has gifted you men. Your suggestions are so appreciated.

Lastly, thank you to my family and friends who kept praying and encouraging me to write this handbook. Your partnership continues to be an incredible blessing. You will never know how much your prayers have helped me in this project.

–Michael J. Peck, D.Min.

Contents

Connecting~Developing Closeness on the Journey of a Lifetime

Introduction *A Word to the Leader:*
Preparing Well to Lead the Sessions 9

Chapter 1 *The Lord Brought You to Me:*
Overcoming the "Two-Ships-in-the-Night" Syndrome 11

Chapter 2 *I Give Myself to You:*
When "For Better or Worse" Really Happens 27

Chapter 3 *How Do I Love You?*
Don't Make it the Best Kept Secret in Town..................................41

Chapter 4 *Wise Ways to Build Bridges:*
One Word You Will Never Forget in Marriage-Building..............59

Chapter 5 *What Makes Closeness Possible?*
Sweetheart, You are Special to Me 75

Chapter 6 *The Leader's Friend:*
Additional Aids & Special Counseling Helps 89

Introduction—A Word to the Leader

Preparing Well to Lead the Sessions

Strong churches and strong marriages are the delight of God.
Both are possible through His Spirit and Word.

"Is any thing too hard for the LORD?" (Genesis 18:14)

Connecting—Developing Closeness on the Journey of a Lifetime is a tool to equip pastors and spiritual leaders to help couples build fresh, dynamic, growing, and connected marriages. This program is part of a series of resources that are biblical in content and practical in application. It is an excellent resource for *all* married couples—whether they are newlyweds or married many years.

As the leader, you can determine how best to present the material and lead the sessions. You can offer this series to just one couple at a time in marriage counseling or present it to a larger audience of couples in a discipleship or Bible study setting. Some pastors may even consider training leaders to present the material in a neighborhood outreach setting.

This *Leader's Edition* will equip you with extra teaching material and notes to assist you in conducting each session. Each chapter was written to complement Dr. Michael Peck's videotaped marriage seminar on the companion DVD. For maximum effectiveness, be sure that each spouse has his or her own copy of the *Couple's Edition*. This will enable each participant to take notes individually during the DVD. The spouses will also complete various homework assignments in their individual workbooks. Though the couples will complete some of the assignments as a couple, in several cases the husbands and wives will be asked to write a few notes in their own guides before the start of each session.

> Each chapter was written to complement Dr. Michael Peck's videotaped marriage seminar on the companion DVD.

You can present the DVD in one of two ways. Your first option is to present each seminar in its entirety. Each session is approximately 40 minutes long. This will provide the biblical teaching on marriage in five sessions. The other option is to select the **Optional conclusion** in each session and thus present the DVD in 10 sessions. The **Optional conclusion** is easy to identify in this *Leader's Edition* and comes complete with material to conclude the current session and begin the following session.

Each chapter begins with a brief list of goals for the session (in the **Goals to consider** section), followed by a brief vignette that presents a couple whose story illustrates the material that will be covered in that session. You will also find **Optional Teaching Points** listed throughout this *Leader's Edition* (and set off in gray-shaded boxes). These provide you with the option of pausing the DVD to share additional information or lead the couple or group in discussion. Your guide also has wide margins for writing additional notes for the session.

Though the names of the couples in the vignettes are fictitious, the stories are a composite of the experiences of real people. Each couple demonstrates typical challenges facing many married couples today. The material presented in the lesson plan not only addresses a specific need but provides the biblical remedy.

At the conclusion of each session's DVD presentation, you will make use of the closing material presented in this guide to emphasize the goal of the session as well as to challenge the couples to make wise and godly decisions. These sections are entitled **Make the most of this moment**. Finally, you will encourage each couple to complete the section entitled **Let's work on connecting this week** before the following session.

> It is my heart-felt prayer that you and your own marriage will be blessed as you encourage dear couples in your neighborhood, ministry, or family to be connecting in their marriages.

It is my heart-felt prayer that you and your own marriage will be blessed as you encourage dear couples in your neighborhood, ministry, or family to be connecting in their marriages. The Lord greatly desires to bless the marriages of both you the leader as well as the couples who attend your sessions. May each of you discover the joy of closeness on the journey of a lifetime! You are not only investing in the lives of couples today but also in the generations to follow.

Chapter 1—The Lord Brought You to Me

Overcoming the "Two-Ships-in-the-Night" Syndrome

Even when separated by miles, our lives are interwoven and
fully connected. My mate may be out of my sight
but never out of my heart.

"Thou hast ravished my heart."
(Song of Solomon 4:9)

Before you present the DVD

Preview the DVD

If time permits, you would be wise to watch all five presentations on the DVD prior to leading this first session. Becoming familiar with the entire scope of the teaching in this series will help you in preparing to lead the sessions. If this is not possible, be sure to view the current session. Decide whether you will present it in its entirety or choose the **Optional conclusion** at the midway point. As you preview the DVD, note the points you want to stress in the margins. It is helpful to read through the *Couple's Edition* to see how their material correlates with the material in your *Leader's Edition* as well as to know ahead of time what their homework will be.

> If time permits, you would be wise to watch all five presentations on the DVD prior to leading this first session. Becoming familiar with the entire scope of the teaching in this series will help you in preparing to lead the sessions.

Goals to consider

While every setting will offer unique challenges and opportunities, you should keep in mind several goals for this first session:

❶ *Assure the couples that they have no need to feel apprehensive about being part of a marriage study group.* It is a common misconception among couples that everyone else's marriage is much better than their own marriage. Couples often mistakenly think that the problems and challenges they face are unique to them and never experienced by others. Assure them that this is *not* the case.

❷ *Seek to provide a relaxed and comfortable setting for your couples.* Assist them in getting to know each other. Do not create a "seminary classroom" setting with this series. Rather, make it enjoyable and relaxed and strive to create an "at home" feeling with each other throughout the series.

❸ *Help the couples to understand God's design for marriage by studying the situation of Adam and Eve.* Challenge your couples to comprehend the situation Adam faced and appreciate the way God provided for him. This will help couples begin to see their marriage in a new light.

❹ *Emphasize the fact that closeness is the characteristic of great marriages.* In this session, you will define closeness and then present the practical applications that result from connecting. Even in good marriages couples can become better connected. It will be exciting to see what the Lord accomplishes through this series and your ministry to the couples.

The couples will meet and think about Bill and Rosie

You will have couples in your seminar very similar to Bill and Rosie.

> You will have couples in your seminar very similar to Bill and Rosie. Their background and early lives were very different.

Their background and early lives were very different. Bill grew up in a small rural community where the handful of neighbors knew each other very well. As the oldest of three siblings, Bill was taught the value of hard work from early childhood. The men in Bill's life worked long hours in strenuous labor.

Bill's father and grandfather were so driven and focused on their work that their families were often neglected. Bill's mother and grandmother often complained about the situation, but nothing changed in their homes. Over the years, they resigned themselves to the fact that though their friends had evenings, vacations, and special times together as families, they would not. Many days Bill's father would not get home from work until the children were in bed.

On those rare occasions when Bill's father was home, he was usually so tired that he wanted nothing more than to sit on the porch and read the paper. When Bill would ask him to go out and throw the ball, go fishing, or spend time with him, his father almost always said "No." The relationship between Bill's parents was strained. They seldom expressed any affection, and fun times in the household were rare.

Rosie was an only child and grew up in a terribly unhappy home. Rosie's mother adamantly insisted that she did not have a drinking problem. But as the years passed, she was more often drunk than sober. Rosie's father usually made excuses for his wife, and though he tried to provide a stable home for Rosie, the alcoholism soon wrought the tragedies so often associated with addiction and abuse.

Rosie's parents' fighting became more frequent and intense. Her mother became more neglectful in caring for her, and a deepening hopelessness grew in her father's heart. As a result, one day Rosie's father announced that he and Rosie were leaving. That day the home was shattered. Though Rosie's father did the best he could, raising his daughter would prove to be a great challenge.

Neither Bill nor Rosie came from a family that knew the Lord and honored the Word of God. But the day the two met at work, almost instantly they were strongly attracted to each other. Casual conversation soon turned to serious talks and even dating. As their interest in each other grew, another emotion was also growing. It was a profound sense of fear. With growing certainty, they knew they wanted to marry each other. But both feared that their marriage would be as unhappy and unfulfilling as their parents' marriages. Neither knew the answer.

Bill and Rosie realized the torment of their parents' marriages and had a great desire for something very different in their own relationship. The couple married nearly a year after their first date. But even though there was no doubt that they loved each other, something was missing. They were not close. The months turned into years.

One morning over breakfast, Bill said to Rosie, "What's missing in our lives? We live under the same roof, share the same mailbox, and have two children, but we are living independently of each other. We just aren't close."

Amazingly enough, a few weeks later a mutual friend invited them to join him at a marriage conference hosted at his church. Bill and Rosie were a little nervous about it, but they accepted the invitation and attended the special services. At that conference they not only learned about knowing Christ in a personal way but together discovered the wonderful joy of what it means to connect in marriage.

Presenting the DVD "The Lord Brought You to Me"

Typically, the couples will prepare for each DVD presentation by reading the introductory material in their *Couple's Editions*. Sometimes the couples will not receive their books before attending this first session. In that case, briefly introduce the presentation by sharing the story of Bill and Rosie.

At this time, open the session with prayer and share any other preliminary information. Remember that you can pause the DVD to share the **Optional teaching**

*At this time, open the session with prayer and share any other preliminary information. Remember that you can pause the DVD to share the **Optional teaching points.** You can also choose either to show the entire DVD (approximately 40 minutes) or to select the **Optional conclusion** at the 26-minute mark.*

points. You can also choose either to show the entire DVD (approximately 40 minutes) or to select the **Optional conclusion** at the 26-minute mark. These decision-points are clearly noted in your *Leader's Edition*.

<u>**Note: The sections underlined in your leader's guide are blanks in the couple's guides to be filled in during the DVD.**</u>

Introduce the DVD by reading the illustration of ships and marriages

In a little red cottage on the Saint Lawrence Seaway, three families with children would camp together for a week each summer. It was the highlight of the entire year. Early morning devotions, lots of freshly baked cookies every day, and close living quarters created rich memories for these families. I know this to be true. My family was one of them!

With deafening shrieks of excitement, the children would come running and shouting, "*Ship! Ship!* Another ship is coming!" Huge ocean-going vessels powered by massive diesel engines would pass so close to the shore that the windows in the little red cottage would rattle. At least once during the week, two massive ships would meet near our little riverside house. What a breathtaking experience it was to watch the ships slowly approach and to hear the deafening air horns sounding out the "captain's salute." Approaching incredibly close, but never touching or connecting, the captains would pilot their ships past each other to continue on their separate voyages.

> Be convinced, it is the plan of the Lord to build marriages characterized by closeness and connection. There is no greater blessing than, as a couple, to become one and to continue to develop closeness in your relationship.

Approaching and recognizing each other with a "captain's salute" of the horn and passing along without connecting is great for ships. However, it is not great for marriages! Why is it that some marriages seem to grow closer and thrive as time passes, and others are more like those two ships that pass in the night as they sail apart on separate voyages?

Be convinced, it is the plan of the Lord to build marriages that are characterized by closeness and connection. There is no greater blessing than, as a couple, to become one and to continue to develop closeness in your relationship.

Start the DVD

How the couples met and their first impression

Marriage really is a journey that God wants to take with you. He truly desires to build closeness in marriage. Overcoming the "two-ships-in-the-night syndrome" is a great work the Lord wants to accomplish in your marriage.

It is interesting to note how couples meet each other. Perhaps you did not meet your mate under the best of circumstances. Regardless of *how* you met, God wants to do amazing and wonderful things in your marriage. What was your first impression of each other?

Imagine what it must have been like for Isaac and Rebekah. Turn to Genesis 24:3-4. Aren't you glad that conditions are very different today? Isaac's marriage was "arranged." His father selected his wife for him! Regardless of the circumstances, God had a plan for Isaac and Rebekah. He has a plan for *your* marriage as well.

We must understand the word "closeness"

(The second and third major points are presented in the next DVD, which focuses on understanding the words "covenant" and "cherish.")

Think of Adam's situation

As we think about closeness in marriage, it is important to lay a good foundation. Married couples today can benefit greatly from studying Genesis 2 and understanding several important things about the first couple, Adam and Eve.

❶ Notice his **placement** (Genesis 2:8b).
What an interesting phrase, "There He put the man whom He had formed." The concept of "putting" actually conveys the idea of setting him down, setting forth, or ordaining that Adam would be there. This was no accident. God had a wonderful plan for Adam, just as He has for you and your marriage today.

❷ Notice his **surroundings** (Genesis 2:8a, 9-15, 19).
It is hard to imagine how beautiful the garden must have been. The words "the LORD God planted a garden eastward in Eden" paint a vivid picture of the beauty and magnificence of Eden. Sin had not yet entered creation. Adam's work was intended to be fun! He had a beautiful garden, enjoyable work, and lots of animals (and not one ferocious!).

❸ Notice his **aloneness and apartness** (Genesis 2:18).
Yet despite the fact that Adam had beautiful surroundings and a fulfilling adventure in the Garden of Eden, something was missing in his life. We do not know how long it took Adam to discover this. He learned that "apartness" was neither pleasant nor beautiful. It was not good. Couples who allow drifting and distance to take place in their relationship likewise discover that "apartness" is not pleasant indeed.

It is helpful to compare verse 18 with verse 20. Though many creatures were nearby, Adam sensed an acute apartness from the animal world. He was alone. The Hebrew word for "alone" means being "solo, apart, and sensing that apartness." Though the garden was beautiful, Adam's life was empty and lonely.

> **Optional Teaching Point—Pause the DVD.**
>
> An important element affecting the couple is their possessions. The place their possessions hold and the value they attach to their possessions have a large bearing on their spiritual focus. While most couples know better, sometimes there is still a strong temptation to think that *things* will make them happy. The opposite is true. Misplaced affection on possessions actually brings sorrow because of the demands of their allegiance as well as shifting their focus from the eternal to the temporal. Consider with the couples these principles concerning their possessions:
>
> - Possessions may turn your attention away from the Lord (Deuteronomy 8:13-14).
> - Possessions can adversely affect your spiritual growth (Mark 4:19).
> - Possessions can be fleeting and are *never* lasting in value (Proverbs 27:24).
> - Possessions can be the wrong focus and purpose for living (1 Timothy 6:9-10).
>
> **After the discussion, resume the DVD.**

Think of God's provision

Two very profound statements taken directly from the Bible play a great role in every marriage that develops closeness. Each couple must apply these statements personally in their own marriage.

> The first statement is found in Genesis 2:18b: "It is not **good** that the man should be **alone;** I will **make** him an **help meet** for him."

After the couples fill in the blanks, they will take a closer look at the statement, focusing on key words and their application. You will direct the couples to circle several key words.

The first word to circle is the word *good*, which means that which is "pleasant, excellent, or beautiful." Generally the idea of the word is that which is beneficial and results in personal pleasure because of the excellence of the situation.

The next word to circle is the word *alone,* which rather dramatically portrays the picture that "others are together, but I am apart. I am alone." There is a sadness or loneliness in this concept. It is imperative for couples to honestly ask themselves, "Are we connected? Is there a closeness between us?"

The last words to circle are the words ***help meet***. Though this is translated as two words in English, in the original Hebrew language it was only one word. The word is *ezer* (pronounced AY-zer) and means "that which fits perfectly and is suitable." Eve fit Adam in a wonderful and complete way.

> The second statement is found in Genesis 2:22: "**Made** He a woman, and **brought** her unto the man."

Sidebar: After the couples fill in the blanks, they will take a closer look at the statement, focusing on key words and their application. You will direct the couples to circle several key words: **good, alone,** and **help meet.**

Direct the couples to circle two words in this section of the study. The first word to circle is **made.** The Scriptures indicate that God formed Adam of the dust of the earth (Genesis 2:7). Eve, however, was not formed. She was made of living tissue from the very spot in Adam's body that was the closest to his heart, one of his ribs. The Hebrew concept of the word *made* is similar to our word "to build." As one would build a house, God literally built a woman from Adam's body, close to his heart.

The second word to circle is **brought.** Following the first surgical procedure ever performed, Adam awoke, and to his great delight God brought Eve to him. The Hebrew word for *brought* means "to present, to introduce." As Adam awoke from surgery, God presented Eve to him and introduced them. From Adam's perspective, she must have been the most beautiful of all the created beings in the garden.

Think of these two statements: "Not good that the man should be alone; I will make him an help meet for him" and "Made he a woman, and brought her unto the man." Couples must view each other as a wonderful gift and cherished blessing from God himself. The Lord can take any couple from right where they are in their marriage relationship and help them to become the couple He desires.

> The Lord can take any couple from right where they are in their marriage relationship and help them to become the couple He desires.

> ### Optional Conclusion—You may stop the DVD here.
> If you choose to conclude the session at this point, use this material as a closing. Stress to the couples the importance of viewing each other as a "help meet." Discuss two or three ways they are a "fit just right" kind of partner in their marriage.
>
> Husbands and wives must be honest both with each other and with themselves. Every couple faces loneliness at times. While marriage partners do not depend solely upon each other to be the source of happiness, God nevertheless intends married couples to connect emotionally, spiritually, and physically. In the next time together couples will look specifically at connecting and how this works in marriage.
>
> ***
>
> If you chose the **Optional conclusion,** then begin the next part of the DVD "The Lord Brought You to Me" by using this material:
>
> We have been thinking about the life of Adam back in the Garden of Eden. Though he lived in the most beautiful of all the places on the earth, something was missing. Even with the sheer pleasure of enjoying his work, something was missing. Though he could walk with the animals, something was missing! He was "alone."
>
> Briefly review the concept of aloneness or apartness as illustrated in the story of Bill and Rosie. Challenge the couples to overcome this disconnect or apartness in their marriage.
>
> **After your opening comments and prayer, resume the DVD.**

Four significant things to know about marriage

From those two profound statements in Genesis 2, we discover four major things that must become significant to us.

> 4 foundational principles flow from the fact that Adam was alone and his aloneness was not good. Marriage is:
> 1. God's idea.
> 2. Honorable.
> 3. One-man and one-woman.
> 4. For one lifetime.

❶ Marriage is **God's idea** (Genesis 2:18).
Never in the history of America has the attack on marriage been greater than it is today. Perhaps the greatest assault comes through the number of couples who ignore marriage altogether or downplay its importance. In 1960, the census indicated that 500,000 unmarried couples were living together in the United States. In 2007, that number had risen to 6.4 million! But even though marriage is ignored by many in our day, it remains God's idea and it still works.

❷ Marriage is **honorable** (Hebrews 13:4).
The word "honorable" comes from the tremendous Greek word *timios* (pronounced TIM-ee-os), meaning "of great price, that which is highly treasured, and therefore very precious." Though He never implies that being single is a second-class state or an undesirable situation, when it comes to the design of marriage, God declares marriage to be honorable.

❸ Marriage is **one-man and one-woman** (Matthew 19:5-6a).
This is an intense connection described by the words "for this cause shall a man leave father and mother, and shall cleave to his wife: and they twain shall be one flesh.... What therefore God hath joined together...." Throughout this series marriage is always considered as one man and one woman brought together in the state of matrimony (following the design of marriage that God established).

❹ Marriage is for **one lifetime** (Matthew 19:6b).
The Lord Jesus was very clear in his statement, "Let not man put asunder." Husbands and wives must never allow anyone or anything to come between them.

These four basic, foundational principles are the outflow of the statements that Adam was alone and that his aloneness was not good. Thus, a help meet would be brought to him. These are the same rock solid principles that all joyfully connected couples embrace in their marriage.

Think of Adam and Eve's condition of being one flesh

Genesis 2:24 states, "And they shall be one flesh." Adam and Eve's condition was one-flesh in nature. This oneness of flesh or closeness conveys the idea that when viewed from a distance the two two spouses are so close that they appear to be one in form. *What a beautiful picture!* This should be the goal of every married couple.

This closeness is best understood as a drawing together, a sense of nearness, a connection *that* we share with no other person or thing. This connection is so practical. It is physical, spiritual, emotional, and sexual. All four aspects are extremely important features of the state of closeness and connecting.

Being married, living together, and even having children does not automatically guarantee closeness and connecting. From this picture of the one-flesh connection, however, we discover several applications for marriage.

Applications for married couples

❶ Decision.
Though often we cannot control our circumstances, we *can* decide to build closeness. This closeness begins with a decision of the will and a purpose of the heart. Together as a couple and individually, husband and wife must decide that this close connection is going to be important and resolve that *it shall be my goal for our marriage.*

> **Optional Teaching Point—Pause the DVD.**
>
> Here is an important opportunity to remind the couples of the importance of making wise decisions and good choices. Focus on the statement, "Often we cannot control our circumstances, but we can build closeness." Sometimes the circumstances are hard. It is sad to see how many marriages fracture when hard times come. Trouble often drives a wedge between husbands who refuse to talk and wives who make decisions based solely upon emotions.
>
> Couples should consider several biblical principles to apply when hard times come:
> - Couples must purpose to really trust the Lord and ask Him to direct their lives (Proverbs 3:5-6).
> - Couples must learn to become confident in the Lord (Proverbs 3:26).
> - Couples must practice casting their heartaches and cares upon Him (Psalm 55:22; 1 Peter 5:7).
> - Couples must determine not to waste time nor miss the lessons God intends for them, even though the trial is hard (1 Peter 1:6-7).
>
> **After the discussion, resume the DVD.**

❷ Experience.
Regardless of the difficulty, couples can overcome "apartness." Every couple will experience many difficult and challenging experiences. In spite of these hardships, however, determined couples truly can experi-

ence the blessing of overcoming difficulties and apartness if they will focus on their partnership and strive to work together in the experiences of life as a married couple.

❸ **Enjoyment**.
Each mate can begin to take steps toward intimacy by becoming totally open with their mate. Though some may not fully understand the exact steps and what the process will involve, wise couples can begin to enjoy even small steps of becoming closer in their relationship.

❹ **Determination**.
This determination is the firm and unshakeable statement, "We are reserved exclusively for the Lord and each other." What a wonderful way to describe your marriage! Do not assume your mate will know this. Your sweetheart will know this by the words you regularly choose and the actions you consistently make.

❺ **Security**.
Security breaks down fear and distrust. Security is the powerful and precious statement that proclaims, "We belong together and with the help of the Lord we will love each other more and more. We will become more closely connected. We will accomplish this because it is God's design."

Declaration of Commitment

Without you, something very precious would be missing in my life.

You make my life complete as a help meet as we are on the journey of our lifetime. I love you very much, and I know that we can grow in our love and devotion to each other.

With the Lord's help, we can overcome any barrier that would hurt our marriage.

We can trust the Lord Jesus to guide us and to travel with us.

So today, I commit to you as my married partner that I will seek to build bridges that will strengthen our marriage as well as to tear down walls that would keep us apart.

Understanding that closeness is the plan of God and the desire of my heart, I am excited about the growing steps of closeness we will take together on this journey of a lifetime.

DVD concludes

Make the most of this moment

As the session comes to a concluding point, make the most of this moment by highlighting several of the key statements from the "Declaration of Commitment." Ask the Lord to give you wisdom (James 1:5) in communicating several important principles for each couple to take home.

Highlight the phrase, **"You make my life complete as a help meet as we are on the journey of a lifetime."** Many couples *assume* their partners know that they are appreciated. Few couples, however, take the time to compile a list of four or five ways their mate really is a help that "fits just right, and is suitable." In your own words, encourage the couples that this will be something they will look forward to completing this week.

Highlight the phrase, **"I commit to you as my married partner that I will seek to build bridges that will strengthen our marriage as well as tear down walls that would keep us apart."** This is a powerful statement. Marriages that are drifting, fractured, and disconnected begin the road to healthy restoration by visualizing these actions and implementing them.

Husbands especially respond to word pictures. Building a bridge and tearing down a wall are both vivid and active. The important truths to grasp focus on the bridges and the walls. What are the ways that the couple can build bridges to reach out and connect? What are some of the walls that keep them apart? These are two things the couple will begin working on this week.

> Husbands especially respond to word pictures. Building a bridge and tearing down a wall are both vivid and active. The important truths to grasp focus on the bridges and the walls.

Let's work on connecting this week

As the leader it is important for you to know exactly what the couple will be working on at home. It is wise for you to read through the *Couple's Edition* and complete the homework for two reasons. First, it will help you prepare for the introduction to the next session. Second, it may help and strengthen your own marriage as well. The following is the material as it is presented in their *Couple's Edition*.

During the next several days, you will have several special assignments to complete both individually and together. These assignments are designed to help you to think honestly about your marriage. It is possible that in the busyness of your lives, the demands of your schedules, and the responsibilities of raising children, your marriage may need some extra attention. This is a special time as you begin to build bridges and tear down walls. The day will come when the last of the children will leave your home. Working on your marriage today and investing in each other now will pay huge dividends in the years to come.

Read the story of Bill and Rosie once again. Think about his statement, "What's missing in our lives? We live under the same roof, share the same mailbox, and have two children, but we are living independently of each other. We just aren't close."

❶ What do you think is meant by the statement, "We are living independently of each other?"

_____
_____
_____
_____
_____
_____
_____
_____

❷ In the DVD session you watched, you learned that although God had placed Adam in the Garden of Eden and surrounded him with beauty and a host of animals, he was alone. There was something missing in his life. According to Genesis 2:18, what did God say about this situation?

_____
_____
_____
_____
_____
_____
_____

❸ God's choice of the words "help meet" is interesting. As you noted in the seminar, a "help meet" is someone who is suitable and fits just right. This does not mean that the "help meet" is perfect. Nor is the "help meet" a mind reader who automatically senses your every whim and responds to your every wish. A "help meet," however, is one who holds a very special position of potential blessing to his or her mate. What are several ways you are a "help meet" to your partner?

What are several ways your mate is a "help meet" to you?

❹ Wonderful marriages do not just happen. They are deliberately built by wise partners who reach out and connect with each other. Closeness takes place in the process of building bridges. List two or three ways you could better reach out to your mate this week.

If you are unsure, would you be willing to quietly and sincerely talk with your mate about this?

❺ Find a time that will work for you and your mate to read the following three passages on three different days this week. Take a few minutes to talk with your mate about each passage and answer the questions together.

Reading #1: Psalm 128

Discuss the wonderful truth of Psalm 128:4 that the blessings of the Lord come to those who reverence or fear Him.

What are some of the blessings you have experienced as a couple? How can you as a couple grow in your reverence for God? What would you say are the five most important things in your marriage and home?

_____
_____
_____
_____
_____
_____
_____

Reading #2: Proverbs 24:1-16

The principles of verses 3-4 will be the focus of conversation for this assignment. The three terms listed in the text are *wisdom*, *understanding*, and *knowledge*. The term *wisdom* has to do with "seeing with discernment." *Understanding* means to "respond with insight." Lastly, *knowledge* is "the demonstration of having a teachable spirit."

By putting these terms into action, you and your mate will be challenged to identify two or three potential or actual walls that could hinder your marriage. Be careful not to place blame. Do not become defensive. By using wisdom, understanding, and knowledge, it will be precious as you and your mate quietly and honestly talk about the walls in your marriage that need to be torn down. **Can you list several walls that need your attention right now?**

_____

_____
_____
_____
_____
_____
_____
_____

Invest some wonderful time holding hands and coming to the Lord in prayer. Ask your heavenly Father to tear down anything that would be a barrier to closeness in your marriage.

Reading #3: Proverbs 10:11-32

This passage sets forth the importance of good communication. Honestly assess the communication level between you and your mate. Wife, do not be surprised if your husband is more or less content with the present level. On the other hand, husbands, don't be surprised if your wife is not satisfied at all. Wives are often much better at communicating than husbands. Good marriages continue to grow as husbands and wives learn to better communicate with each other.

Your assignment for day three is to do something together that will provide time for you both to talk and honestly share with each other. You may decide to go for a walk and hold hands. Maybe you will make a lunch date together. Some may prefer to sit on a park bench and communicate. Be creative and make the time memorable.

This communication could include reminiscing, sharing how much you mean to each other, talking about your future hopes and dreams, as well as talking about the goodness of the Lord. Together count some of the many ways God has blessed you.

Really determine that you will be willing to do your part in building bridges and tearing down the walls that we will target in later sessions. Now is the time to start working on these.

Before the next DVD session, be sure to read the story of Jim and Sheila in chapter 2.

Additional things the Lord is teaching me

Chapter 2—I Give Myself to You

When "For Better or Worse" Really Happens

How marvelous this deepest mystery, to discover joy in the giving of myself to my sweetheart, on the good days as well as on the bad!

"My beloved is mine, and I am his...."
(Song of Solomon 2:16)

Before you present the DVD

Your couples now return for the next step in building closeness. For some this may be the first time they have really worked on developing closeness by connecting. Hopefully, they have taken their homework seriously and begun to really communicate, invested time with the Lord and each other through Bible reading, and enjoyed doing something together.

> Your couples now return for the next step in building closeness. For some this may be the first time they have really worked on developing closeness by connecting.

Preview the DVD

Once again you will determine whether to show the entire DVD or select the **Optional conclusion**. As you preview the DVD, note the points you want to stress in the margins. It is helpful to read through the *Couple's Edition* to see how their material correlates with your *Leader's Edition* as well as to know ahead of time what their homework will be.

Goals to consider

While every setting will offer unique challenges and opportunities, you should keep in mind several goals for this session:

❶ *Select several things to use from the previous homework to begin this session.* You may ask if anyone would like to share how the Lord has used His Word this week to work in their lives.

❷ *Two keys words, **covenant** and **cherishing**, will be presented in this session.* These words will build on the word closeness from the last session. Communicate clearly the difference between a legal contract and the incredible covenant marriage couples have made.

❸ *Alert the couples that two wonderful ingredients for dynamic marriages will be presented in a few moments.* These essential ingredients are represented by the words *love* and *cherish*. Ask the couples to take just a minute to begin thinking about how these two words complement each other.

> Alert the couples that two wonderful ingredients for dynamic marriages will be presented in a few moments. These essential ingredients are represented by the words *love* and *cherish*.

The couples will meet and think about Jim and Sheila

(Your couples should have read this story before coming to the session.)

> Jim and Sheila were childhood playmates. Soon after Jim turned six, his family moved into the community in which Sheila's family lived. Small communities do not offer a large selection of friends from which to choose, and thus Jim and Sheila and the two or three other children their age made up the little band of youngsters that played together nearly every day.
>
> Sheila did not especially like Jim as a child. He was always finding ways to get dirty! Jim thought Sheila was a sissy little princess who was always afraid of getting smudged or breaking her little fingernails. But since there were few other options, the two played together with their friends and at least put up with each other. All that changed in the middle of their senior year of high school, however, when suddenly Jim and Sheila noticed each other in a totally different way.
>
> After Jim graduated from college a few years later, the two married in the only church in town. Jim was accepted as a junior partner in a business across the state, and so Jim and Sheila moved into their apartment and immediately became busy in life. Jim's supervisors gave their young partner extra assignments, and Jim, eager to impress his supervisors, consistently accepted more and more work.
>
> Sheila worked part-time in a department store downtown. Her flexible hours were a great help after the birth of their first child. Before they knew it, a second child was born … and then a third. Over the next several years, Jim's role in his company expanded and, with it, his hours and responsibilities. Sheila began to resent the many hours Jim was away from home. She hated the tension that was growing, but she just didn't know what to do about it.
>
> Several times they talked about their lives and marriage. Neither was happy about the long hours of work and demanding schedules. Both readily admitted that the closeness they had once enjoyed was gone. Both confessed that they took each other for granted, and Jim even said that he understood why Sheila felt the way she described. Almost in dejection, they con-

cluded that this was the way their marriage would be for the rest of their lives.

One day, though, a single telephone call turned their lives upside-down. Sheila answered, and a very concerned young doctor from the local hospital asked, "Do you have someone who can bring you to the ER? I don't want you coming alone. Your husband has been injured in a car crash on the interstate. His injuries are very serious."

Suddenly the room seemed to be whirling in all directions. Sheila phoned the couple next door and they came to the rescue. While the wife stayed with the children, the husband quickly drove Sheila to the hospital and stayed with her. The news was grim. Jim was being prepared for emergency surgery. Sheila had just a second to kiss her unconscious husband goodbye before he was whisked down the hall to the waiting elevator.

Will this be the last time I see my husband alive? she wondered. Beside herself, she collapsed and sobbed in the waiting room. Her neighbor said, "I hope you don't mind, but I called my pastor and he is on the way." At that moment Sheila was too weak to object to anything. Her world had suddenly changed. She realized then that Jim was far more important to her than she had shown in the way she had been treating him. Now she could lose him without having the chance to tell him how much she truly loved him. That thought was devastating.

Over the next several weeks, Jim slowly began to recover. The visits and counsel of the pastor, as well as the kindness of her neighbors, were indescribably helpful. On day 18 in the hospital, during one of the pastor's many visits, Jim and Sheila both placed their trust in the Lord Jesus for salvation. The pastor was genuinely thrilled and assured them that he would be there to help them grow in their new-found faith in Christ.

Jim and Sheila both knew that their lives were in for dramatic changes. Before leaving, the pastor turned and stood at the door of Jim's room and said, "It is amazing how the Lord caught your attention and has given you another chance to build a close marriage. Many couples will never experience what you two have been through. Don't waste this great opportunity. Be deliberate in doing something every day to draw closer to each other."

Before the pastor waved goodbye and slipped out of the room, Jim took Sheila's *hand* and quietly said, "Don't worry, Pastor, I will be deliberate." Though their marriage did not change overnight, it was never the same. Jim and Sheila learned to be deliberate in viewing their marriage in a totally different light.

> The pastor told Jim and Sheila: "Don't waste this great opportunity. Be deliberate in doing something every day to draw closer to each other."

You may wish to review the story of Jim and Sheila as a good way to introduce the DVD.

Presenting the DVD "I Give Myself To You"

Typically, the couples will prepare for each DVD presentation by reading the introductory material. If some have not done so, briefly introduce the presentation by sharing the story of Jim and Sheila.

At this time, open the session with prayer and share any other preliminary information. Remember that you can pause the DVD to share the **Optional teaching points.** You can also choose either to show the entire DVD (approximately 44 minutes) or to select the **Optional conclusion** at the 15-minute mark. These decision-points are clearly noted in your *Leader's Edition*.

<u>Note: **The sections underlined in your leader's guide are blanks in the couple's guides to be filled in during the DVD.**</u>

> Remember that you can pause the DVD to share the **Optional teaching points.** You can also choose either to show the entire DVD (approximately 44 minutes) or to select the **Optional conclusion** at the 15-minute mark.

Introduce the DVD by reading the illustration of the marriage vows

Most couples enjoy thinking about their wedding day. Take a moment with the couples to recall the significance of their vows. You may wish to share something about your own wedding and the joy you experienced in pledging your heart and life to your mate. Most couples will remember the excitement they shared in getting married.

It is possible that one or more couples are living together without being married. Try to be sensitive to this situation and ask the Lord to give you great wisdom as you work with these couples.

> It is possible that one or more couples are living together without being married. Try to be sensitive to this situation and ask the Lord to give you great wisdom as you work with these couples.

In this session, couples will be thinking specifically about the "for better or worse" in their vows and the promise to "love, honor, and cherish." These are far more than merely clauses in a contract. The true depth of the relationship between the husband and wife is actually that of a *covenant*, a pledging of one's life to another.

As the leader, be sure to prayerfully seize this great opportunity to invest in the lives of your couples. Some may not clearly understand the meaning of the words or the concepts of *closeness* and *covenant*. This session provides a great opportunity to build closeness in marriage.

Start the DVD

A note that is humorous and sad

Humor and sorrow do not typically belong in the same sentence. In this case, however, the words are both funny and very sad. This little story surely illustrates the truth that words sometimes do not really convey the heart's attitude.

Framed in a beautifully crafted wooden frame was a picture of a couple who was obviously happy and apparently deeply in love. On the back of the picture were the words: "I love you with all of my heart, and would do anything in the world for you. I would swim the widest ocean, and scale the highest mountain. I will love you forever." The photo was signed, and though the wording was a bit strange, to the couple in the picture the statement obviously meant romance. Then came the P.S. that read: "If we should break up, I would like the frame back again." Somehow, the tender moment of lasting love was lost in that horrific additional note.

The promise of doing anything in the world—swimming the widest ocean and scaling the highest mountain—suddenly meant little when cast beside the statement of wanting the frame back if the marriage broke up. Promises built on empty words are of little value. But love honestly expressed by words *and* backed up with confirming actions is a rare and precious treasure.

Most of us would never dream of saying something so devastating to our partner, but many couples act out what that P.S. was saying. How do wise couples overcome situations that would tend to drive them apart?

In the first DVD session, we discussed the Lord's wonderful intention by understanding the word *closeness*. Now let's continue the study.

We must understand the word "covenant"

Direct the couples to turn to Malachi 2:14 in their Bibles. In this passage the Old Testament prophet pleaded with the people. He especially targeted the fracturing of marriages. It is heartbreaking to see how quickly some husbands were divorcing their wives in Malachi's day. He called on them (and on *us*) to view their wives as partners in the covenant.

The two views of marriage

Understanding marriage and what it truly means will greatly impact couples. There are basically two ways of viewing the marriage relationship.

> There are basically two ways of viewing the marriage relationship:
> - As a **contract**.
> - As a **covenant**.

❶ Some incorrectly view marriage as a **contract**.
Contracts are generally conditional and often have a wide variety of loopholes and contingencies. Contracts are established to help people safely enter into agreements with other parties. If the second party agrees to follow the stipulations, then the first party agrees likewise to fulfill his part. Contracts provide contingencies in the event that either party fails to follow the written promises and thus breaches the contract. Marriage is *not* a contract.

❷ Malachi correctly viewed marriage as a **covenant**.

A *covenant* is a lasting pledge in which one gives oneself unconditionally and totally to another. It is the pledging of one's life and being to the other.

> **Optional Teaching Point—Pause the DVD.**
>
> Seize the moment and opportunity to emphasize the concept *unconditional*. It literally presents the powerful truth of giving oneself without conditions and clauses. It is best understood as pledging oneself to another and giving oneself to the marriage partner totally and freely.
> - This is a beautiful picture of the grace of the Lord Jesus Christ, who in His great love totally gave Himself to the believer (Galatians 2:20).
> - The unconditional aspect of the covenant demonstrates a life of commitment and devotion in spite of circumstances. Married couples have pledged their lives to each other when times are better or worse. This provides a wonderful illustration of the *agape* love that seeks the welfare of those who may not deserve it and who may not return it. Key verses that illustrate this powerful love include John 3:16, Romans 5:8, and 1 John 4:10-11.
>
> **After the discussion, resume the DVD.**

Never forget the difference between a contract and covenant. *Marriage is **not** a contract. It is a covenant.* There are no loopholes or contingencies in marriage.

> Never forget the difference between a contract and covenant. *Marriage is not a contract. It is a covenant.* There are no loopholes or contingencies in marriage.

This is powerful because couples pledge their lives to each other. Of all the life-long agreements into which people may enter, marriage is the greatest because it involves the pledging of their life and being as a gift presented to their mate.

This is very personal. From a human perspective, you are pledging that which is precious to another. With the exceptions of our relationship to the Lord and the relationship of parent and child, no other human relationship compares. No amount of money, possessions, or other promises come close by comparison to personally pledging one's life to one's mate.

This covenant is *intentional*. Wise and godly couples live out the covenant aspect of their marriage on a daily basis. Never assume that your mate knows this. Be intentional in the way you live every day.

> **Key principle:** I must live in such a way as to communicate this decision of my heart in <u>attitudes, actions, and affection</u>.

> **Optional Conclusion—You may stop the DVD here.**
>
> If you choose to conclude the session at this point, use this material as a closing. Stress to the couples the importance of viewing each other from the perspective of the covenant. Pledging one's life to another is profoundly significant. Every couple will experience disagreements, annoyances, and perhaps even deep hardships on their journey of a lifetime. The covenant aspect of marriage, however, understands that this relationship is enduring. Couples have pledged themselves to their mates.
>
> **
>
> If you chose the **Optional conclusion**, then begin the next part of the DVD "I Give Myself To You" by using this material.
>
> In our last session together we reviewed the difference between a contract and a covenant. Do you remember the difference? A contract is a conditional statement that may or may not have contingencies and loopholes. A covenant is very different from this, as it is unconditional and involves the total giving of myself to my mate. Marriage is a wonderful covenant that finds joy in giving ourselves totally and unconditionally to each other.
>
> Today, we will continue to explore several key concepts beyond the words *closeness* (in our first session) and *covenant* (in our previous session).
>
> **After your opening comments and prayer, resume the DVD.**

We must understand the word "cherish"

Direct the couples to turn to Malachi 2:14. Though this was written during the Old Testament era, Malachi's statement provides wonderful principles for us to grasp. In a wonderful way, Malachi spotlights emotional attachment with the concept of *cherishing*.

Next, direct the couples to turn to Proverbs 5:15-21. In a vivid and descriptive manner, the author of Proverbs details the joy experienced in the shared sexual relationship of couples who cherish each other. The one who cherishes his or her mate will not look for any other with whom to share his or her love.

> Direct the couples to turn to Proverbs 5:15-21. In a vivid and descriptive manner, the author of Proverbs details the joy experienced in the shared sexual relationship of couples who cherish each other.

Two special words

In most wedding services, the marriage vows involve the words "to have and to hold from this day forward, in sickness and in health, for better or worse, richer or poorer, to love and to cherish until death do us part."

❶ Focus on the word **_love_**.

> **Love:**
> The biblical concept of love is far beyond a mere emotional feeling. Love really is *a decision of my will* that I will unconditionally seek the well-being of my mate.

The biblical concept of love is far beyond a mere emotional feeling. Love really is *a decision of my will* that I will unconditionally seek the well-being of my mate. Love certainly involves romance, tenderness, and friendship. But it is vitally important that couples understand that biblical love is a *decision of the will* that I will invest in my mate by seeking his or her well-being.

Optional Teaching Point—Pause the DVD.

This may be a good point to pause the DVD and ask the couples to focus on John 3:16 and Romans 5:8. Both verses reveal the great, unconditional love of God poured out to those who did not deserve it. This love is known as *agape* love.

As you explain these verses, this is an excellent opportunity to share the Gospel with the couples. It is possible that there may be some in attendance who do not know the Lord as Savior.

After the discussion, resume the DVD.

❷ Focus on the word **cherish**.

> **Cherish:**
> To cherish another basically means to hold dear, to treat with tenderness, to treasure, and to value. This is a precious way to view your mate. It is the standard God has established to describe a healthy marriage.

To *cherish* another basically means to hold dear, to treat with tenderness, to treasure, and to value. This is a precious way to view your mate. It is the standard God has established to describe a healthy marriage.

The concepts of loving and cherishing our mate provide the key to discovering the joy of closeness on the journey of a lifetime. Wise couples are very careful not to take each other for granted.

When the words "covenant" and "cherish" are understood together, feelings of entrapment and hardship should diminish. Difficult times will come and there will always be obstacles to overcome. But when couples understand their marriage as being a covenant in which they cherish each other, their relationship is blessed indeed despite hardship and tribulation.

Three necessary things that must take place

❶ Make sure the Lord has **His rightful place**.

Regardless of the personalities in your marriage, and your personal experiences, the Lord must have first-place in your home and marriage. When He is given His rightful place, you will enjoy His blessings. This does not mean that everything will be quick, easy, and happy. It *does* mean that even in the difficult times, He will bless the lives and marriages of those who give Him His rightful place.

Recall what Moses told Joshua to tell the people in Deuteronomy 6:5-6: *"And thou shalt love the LORD thy God with all thine heart, and with all thy soul, and with all thy might. And these words, which I command thee this day, shall be in thine heart."* The people were to give God His rightful place. At the end of his life, Joshua had not forgotten that command. In Joshua 24:15 he declared, *"And if it seem evil unto you to serve the LORD, choose you this day whom ye will serve...but as for me and my house, we will serve the LORD."*

❷ Determine to **resolve conflicts and overcome any obstacles**.

Most conflicts and obstacles begin as minor annoyances that are allowed to grow and fester. Wise couples address these situations lovingly and quickly before they grow into big issues.

❸ Learn how to both **give and receive love unconditionally**.

If you grew up in an unhappy home, perhaps you are finding it difficult to receive love and express it. Marriages that are genuinely close and connected are those that both give and receive love *unconditionally*.

Four ways these blessings are demonstrated

❶ This will be demonstrated by your **walk with the Lord**.

This has to do with the way you live for the Lord and have an ongoing fellowship with Him as expressed in Ephesians 4:1 where we are commanded, *"I therefore, the prisoner of the Lord, beseech you that ye walk worthy of the vocation wherewith ye are called."*

❷ This will be demonstrated by your **attitudes and actions**.

Actions are closely connected to your attitude. The way you think of your mate, as well as the way you treat him or her, reveals the condition of your heart (and often the health of your marriage).

❸ This will be demonstrated by the **value you place on your mate**.

How do you express to your mate the great value you place on him or her? This is especially important because of who he or she is—not just because of what he or she does. You must value your mate as a person you cherish.

❹ This will be demonstrated by your **devotion**.

Your devotion speaks of the level of carefulness and regard you have for your mate. You must be committed totally to your sweetheart and marriage. This is not overbearing, entrapment, or confinement. It certainly is

Blessings are demonstrated in 4 main ways:
1. Walking with the Lord.
2. Attitudes and actions.
3. Valuing your mate.
4. Devotion to your mate.

not an obsession. It is helping your mate to know that, next to the Lord, he or she is the most important person in your life.

DVD concludes

Make the most of this moment

> Your couples are challenged to take significant steps this week by communicating unconditional love to each other because they are cherished. **This is a significant moment to emphasize the truth of John 13:17** where the Lord Jesus said, "If ye know these things, happy are ye if ye do them."

The DVD presentation concludes in a tender way. Your couples are challenged to take significant steps this week by communicating unconditional love to each other because they are cherished. This is a significant moment to emphasize the truth of John 13:17 where the Lord Jesus said, "If ye know these things, happy are ye if ye do them."

Emphasize that the Lord greatly desires to help us develop closeness with our mate. This will begin to take place when we recognize that our marriage is a covenant and that our mate is to be cherished. Encourage your couples to take this seriously, as you as their leader do as well.

Let's work on connecting this week

As the leader it is important for you to know exactly what the couple will be working on at home. It is wise for you to read through the *Couple's Edition* and complete the homework for two reasons. First, it will help you prepare for the introduction to the next session. Second, it may help and strengthen your own marriage as well. The following is the material as it is presented in their *Couple's Edition*.

During the next several days, you will have several special assignments to complete both individually and together as a couple. These assignments are designed to help you to think honestly about your marriage. It is possible that in the "busyness" of your lives, the demands of your schedules, and the responsibilities of raising children, your marriage may need some extra attention. The homework this week will focus on the significance of the terms *covenant* and *cherishing*.

Read again the story of Jim and Sheila and answer several questions from their story.

❶ What did it take for Jim and Sheila to make some dramatic changes in the way they viewed each other?

_____

_____

_____

❷ Before the pastor left Jim's hospital room, he encouraged Jim and Sheila to be deliberate in doing something specific. What was it?

❸ What are several things you could do to be deliberate in expressing this to your mate?

❹ Please read Ephesians 5:21-33. What are several ways the godly wife can demonstrate to her husband that she cherishes him?

_____
_____
_____
_____
_____

What are several ways the godly husband can demonstrate to his wife that he cherishes her?

_____
_____
_____
_____
_____
_____
_____
_____
_____

❺ For this part of the homework, you and your mate will exchange books. Each will express their love and let the spouse know he or she is cherished. (Though some may find writing difficult, take the time to prayerfully and carefully write a few sentences to communicate your love for your partner and why you cherish him or her as your beloved one. Some may want to write out a "rough draft" of their note on a scrap paper first.)

To my partner, from my heart I want to say:

_____
_____
_____
_____
_____
_____
_____

When both of you have completed this part of the assignment, return your partner's copy and read his or her note. Make this a tender moment. Take time to pray with each other and thank the Lord for your marriage partner.

Be sure to be working on your walk with the Lord. Seek to be in God's Word daily and invest some time with Him in prayer. If you are not in the habit of reading the Bible every day, start now. A good place to begin reading is the book of Ephesians. Read a chapter each day and see the greatness of the Lord Jesus Christ. Ask Him what He desires for you to see and learn about Him every day.

Be very deliberate in expressing to your mate that you love and cherish him or her. Likewise, be very deliberate in watching for such expressions from your mate. If this does not happen at first, however, commit it to the Lord and ask Him to help you respond appropriately and lovingly. Be sure to be expressing love in your words, actions, and attitudes this week. Deliberately focus on connecting with your mate and developing closeness on the journey of a lifetime.

> Remind the couples to be sure to read the story of Mark and Samantha in chapter 3 before the next session.

Before the next DVD session, be sure to read the story of Mark and Samantha in chapter 3.

Additional things the Lord is teaching me

_____
_____
_____
_____
_____
_____
_____
_____
_____
_____
_____
_____
_____
_____
_____
_____

Chapter 3—How Do I Love You?

Don't Make it the Best-Kept Secret in Town!

There is no greater blessing than to marry the one who is not only the love of my life, but who also becomes my very best friend.

"This is my beloved, and this is my friend."
(Song of Solomon 5:16)

Before you present the DVD

In this session, your couples will discover the vital importance of expressing their love through actions and deliberately developing closeness through togetherness. Hopefully they have taken their homework seriously and begun to really communicate, invested time with the Lord and each other through Bible reading, and enjoyed doing something together.

Preview the DVD

Once again you will determine whether to show the entire DVD or select the **Optional conclusion**. As you preview the DVD, note the points you want to stress in the margins. It is helpful to read through the *Couple's Edition* to see how their material correlates with your *Leader's Edition* as well as to know ahead of time what their homework will be.

> As you preview the DVD, note the points you want to stress in the margins. It is helpful to read through the couple's guide to see how their material correlates to your leader's guide as well as to know ahead of time what their homework will be.

Goals to consider

While every setting will offer unique challenges and opportunities, you should keep in mind several goals for this session:

❶ *Help the couples overcome the temptation of assuming their mates know of their love.* Connecting takes place when love is freely broadcast and received in marriage.

❷ *The concept of **togetherness** will be presented in this session. Make it a prayerful goal that couples will appreciate this blessing and make it real in their marriage.*

❸ *Help the couples discover the importance of how closeness develops through the key concepts that they must consistently apply in their lives.*

The couples will meet and think about Mark and Samantha

(Your couples should have read this story before coming to the session.)

> On the surface, and in public, Mark and Samantha's marriage seems to be ideal. Yet at home the conflicts that result from their contrasting personalities is producing serious friction.

Mark and his wife Samantha seem to have a really good marriage. Everyone views them as a sweet couple who achieved success early in life. If the saying is true that opposites attract, it is no wonder that Mark and Samantha were so strongly attracted to each other.

Highly motivated, Mark carries on the family business with a zest that would make his grandfather and father very proud. A gifted administrator, Mark is very organized and logical in his decision-making. At times he can appear rather cold and insensitive and even a little angry when situations and people inconvenience him.

Samantha, on the other hand, is very outgoing. She is often the life of the party. Give her a few minutes and she can have a whole roomful of guests in laughter. Organization has never been one of her strong points. She tends to speak before she thinks and sometimes makes promises she cannot keep.

On the surface, and in public, their marriage seems to be ideal. Yet at home the conflicts that result from their contrasting personalities is producing serious friction. Mark wants the home clean and orderly. Samantha copes well in clutter, and does not see why this should be such an issue. Mark is well-organized in his business and expects Samantha to run the home in the same way. Samantha sees the joy and humor in situations and expects Mark to be more fun when he comes home.

The tension continues to build. Finally, one night in a cold and insensitive outburst, as Mark steps into the house from work, he blurts, "Sam, for goodness sake, this place is a mess! What in the world have you done all day? I want my home clean and in order. Is that too much to ask?"

Samantha is crushed and infuriated at the same time. How dare he question what she did all day? In addition to home-schooling their children, she baked and delivered a cherry pie to the shut-in across town. She phoned three people in three different hospitals to brighten their day. Not to mention that she wrote to one of the missionary families who was experiencing hard times on the field.

They rapidly hurled strong and unpleasant words at one another. Samantha labeled Mark as "cold and unappreciative." Mark fired back that Samantha was "disorganized and disastrous at home." The wounds were hot and stinging. Sadly, though what Mark and Samantha each said contained elements of truth, their personalities were out of control and their conversation was unloving.

They ate supper in silence. Their three children, ages 7, 5, and 3, looked at their parents and then at each other. No one at the table was happy. Mark consumed his food without even tasting it. Samantha cried several times.

As soon as supper was finished, Samantha sarcastically said, "Let me quickly get these dishes done so your house will be perfect." Mark, very unwisely, replied, "It will take more than doing these few dishes to accomplish *that*."

A few minutes after supper was finished, the phone rang. It was Grandma calling to talk with her grandchildren. When 7-year-old Tommy came to the phone, Mark and Samantha heard him say, "Grandma, I wish you were here. Mommy and Daddy were mean to each other. I think they hate each other. Dad thinks Mommy is lazy and makes a mess. Mommy thinks Dad is mean. I think Mommy and Daddy both need to sit in the time-out chair."

Suddenly, Mark and Samantha felt as though a ton of bricks had hit them. Samantha grabbed the phone and assured her mother that everything was all right. After listening to her mother's wise counsel, Samantha quietly said, "You are right, Mom. Thanks for the encouragement. We will talk later tonight. I love you."

Later that night, after the children were in bed, Mark and Samantha were both calm, quiet, and very ashamed of the way they had acted earlier in the day. Sitting next to Mark on the couch, Samantha quietly cried and asked Mark to forgive her for the way she had been living and keeping their home. Her words, "Mark, I never meant to be a disappointment to you," immediately brought deep remorse to Mark for his attitudes and actions.

Crushed by the way he had wounded his wife, Mark choked out, "How could I have treated you so terribly? Can you ever forgive me?" Sobbing, Mark was not only sorry for the way he had treated Sammy but he was also angry at himself for the coldness and sarcasm with which he had treated her.

That night was a turning point. As they talked into the late hours of the night, Mark and Samantha both once again pledged their love to one another. Both purposed in their hearts that they would be aware of the weak areas of their personalities as well as the potential conflicts. It would be interesting to see how their pledges live out in the months and years to come.

> "Grandma, I wish you were here. Mommy and Daddy were mean to each other. I think they hate each other. Dad thinks Mommy is lazy and makes a mess. Mommy thinks Dad is mean. I think Mommy and Daddy both need to sit in the time-out chair."

> One of the commitments Mark and Samantha pledged to each other was that they would return to having devotions together regularly, speak kindly to each other, find a way to communicate their love daily in little practical ways, share some of the chores around the house, share more time together, and encourage each other daily. Their children soon saw the difference.
> A few weeks later, Tommy was overheard telling Grandma on the phone, "Don't worry, Grandma. Mom and Dad love each other again. I caught them kissing in the kitchen. It almost made me sick." (Remember, he is 7!)

You may wish to review the story of Mark and Samantha as a good way to introduce the DVD.

Presenting the DVD "How Do I Love You?"

Typically, the couples will prepare for each DVD presentation by reading the introductory material. If some have not done so, briefly introduce the presentation by sharing the story of Mark and Samantha.

At this time, open the session with prayer and share any other preliminary information. Remember that you can pause the DVD to share the **Optional teaching points.** You can also choose either to show the entire DVD (approximately 45 minutes) or to select the **Optional conclusion** at the 22-minute mark. These decision-points are clearly noted in your *Leader's Edition*.

<u>**Note: The sections underlined in your leader's guide are blanks in the couple's guides to be filled in during the DVD.**</u>

Introduce the DVD by reading the illustration of being on the journey

Most couples have taken a journey at least once in their lifetime. To ensure a successful journey, before embarking on such a trip, the couple makes plans and maps out the route they will take. Those who travel know that they will encounter a wide variety of experiences on the journey. There will likely be long uphill climbs and steep descents, twists and turns, and even an unpleasant pothole to negotiate here and there. All these are to be expected on such a journey. The journey will bring many variations along the way.

Marriage is very similar.... It, too, is a journey—a journey that lasts a lifetime. The Lord greatly desires to assist His children on this journey. He delights in helping couples grow and mature. What a great testimony it is when two people with two different backgrounds and personalities learn the joy of connecting as they develop closeness on the journey of a lifetime!

Sidebar: Remember that you can pause the DVD to share the **Optional teaching points.** You can also choose either to show the entire DVD (approximately 45 minutes) or to select the **Optional conclusion** at the 22-minute mark.

Start the DVD

The three things we share in common

1. Every couple has a **past**.

2. Every couple has **personalities**.

3. Every couple has **problems**.

Regardless of these three things, the Lord desires husbands and wives to genuinely love each other. He does not want you to assume your mate knows this. In a marvelous way, the Lord expresses His love both in word and actions. With this in mind, married couples must express their love in word and in action. Closeness and connecting will build as love is communicated and received.

The declaration of what must take place

In Matthew 19:5-6, the Lord Jesus explains how one man and one woman for one lifetime is the plan of God. See the five key concepts below and understand that these essential elements are necessary if you are going to connect with your mate.

1. Understand the word **leave**.

    When the Lord speaks of leaving father and mother, it is not an action of abandonment. Rather, the idea means to **loosen, to let go**. You must not be bound to your parents as you were when you lived in their home as a child.

2. Understand the power of **cleave**.

    As you loosen the tie that bound you to your parents, a new relationship takes place in cleaving to your mate. The idea of cleaving means to **glue and stick together**.

    Cleaving is a picture of two boards being glued so tightly together that it is impossible to separate them without causing great damage. What an incredible picture the Lord uses to describe the relationship that marriage partners should be enjoying.

3. Understand the concept of **two shall be one**.

    How incredible it is to understand that in the plan of the all-wise God you and your mate are declared to be *one!* This oneness includes the act of sexual intimacy as well as the emotional connection with your mate. This wonderful connection continues to grow in time.

4. Understand the statement of what **God has joined together**.

    While it may be hard to picture today, this joining together is best under-

> Five key concepts are essential elements for connecting with your mate:
> 1. Leave.
> 2. Cleave.
> 3. Two shall be one.
> 4. God joined together.
> 5. Put asunder.

stood as being in the yoke together. The yoke is the ancient device that kept the oxen joined (or bound together) in step and in place as they worked together. Though this may sound strange, it is a beautiful picture of the blessing of being held joyously together in the plan of God.

> **Optional Teaching Point—Pause the DVD.**
>
> This may provide you as the leader a great opportunity to further expound on the way the Lord Jesus uses the picture of the yoke, and our relationship with Him. This classic teaching is found in Matthew 11:28-30.
>
> The yoke speaks of the wonderful partnership between the Lord and His people. This partnership is just one of the many blessings of salvation.
>
> **After the discussion, resume the DVD.**

❺ Understand the danger or the possibility of ***put asunder***.

Godly couples must be on guard never to allow anyone or anything to separate or push them apart from their mate.

Apply these principles as husband and wife

3 things every couple must understand:
1. Never become careless.
2. Be aware of what would pull you apart.
3. Do that which will draw you together.

There are three things every couple must understand. These are basic and foundational in nature and are essential to building a successfully connected marriage. As a couple, be sure you are taking steps to apply these to your marriage. The use of the word *we* means that both the husband and the wife must take these matters seriously and apply them in three powerful ways.

❶ We must never **become careless**.

As it is dangerous to become careless in our driving, so it is dangerous to become careless in our marriage. You can never place too high a view or value on your marriage.

❷ We must beware of anyone or anything that might **pull us apart**.

Couples who begin to slowly drift apart open the door to becoming emotionally attached to someone other than their mate. This is an extremely dangerous situation because it often begins rather innocently. Left unchecked, this emotional attachment can quickly grow into a deeper relationship that can lead to unfaithfulness and heartache.

❸ We must determine to do everything that will **draw us together**.

This does not mean you will be with your mate 24 hours a day. It does not mean that couples cannot do things separately from time to time. It does mean, however, that you and your mate deliberately choose to invest in each other, encourage each other, and, by your words and actions, allow yourself to become attached emotionally, physically, and sexually with each other.

Key Principle: We can and we really must connect with our partner. It is God's plan for successful marriages.

> **Optional Conclusion—You may stop the DVD here.**
>
> If you choose to conclude the session at this point, use this material as a closing. Wise couples understand that marriages either grow closer and deeper in connection or they will slowly drift apart. The next session of viewing the DVD "How Do I Love You?" will present very practical material that shares specific ways to deepen the marriage connection.
>
> The idea of cleaving has been presented today. You become glued to your mate by several significant factors.
> - Your relationship and fellowship with Christ
> - Your words of endearment and appreciation
> - Your actions of thoughtfulness, respect, and devotion
>
> This week, it is important to think about these three major factors in your personal life. It would be wise to jot down a note or two about all three of these areas and how you can improve and grow in each.
>
> **
>
> If you choose the **Optional conclusion** then begin the next viewing of the DVD "How Do I Love You?" with the following material. Review the marriage of Mark and Samantha. Make a note of their personalities and how they clashed. Also point out the seriousness that results when personalities are out of control and harm not only on the marriage but the children as well.
>
> Prepare the couples by challenging them to honestly talk with each other about the weaknesses and strengths of their personalities. Encourage them to focus on the one-flesh concept and how the Lord desires to help His people to become glued to, or connected, in every way to their mate.
>
> **After your opening comments and prayer, resume the DVD at this point.**

Key Principle: We can and we really must connect with our partner. It is God's plan for successful marriages.

The demonstration of what must be shown

You must never assume that your mate knows of your love. *Genuine love must be genuinely demonstrated.* Are you consistently and tenderly communicating your love and devotion?

Romans 5:8 is the announcement that God does not want us to merely *assume* He loves us. Clearly the Lord demonstrates His love by His words and actions. Paul the Apostle declares, "But God commendeth his love toward us, in that, while we were yet sinners, Christ died for us." The word *commendeth* literally means that God boldly proclaims His love and clearly demonstrates it by His actions.

Understand the various dimensions of genuine love

The early Greeks had several words to describe the various aspects of love. When you fully and totally love your mate in the way the Lord intended, you will develop and enjoy these five expressions of love in your marriage.

> The early Greeks had several words to describe the various aspects of love:
> 1. Phileo.
> 2. Eros.
> 3. Storge.
> 4. Epithumeo.
> 5. Agape.

❶ The expression of **_phileo_ love, which means _friendship_**.

In John 11:36, the Jewish people at the graveside of Lazarus noted, "Behold how He loved him!" The word for love expressed in this verse is characterized as a precious friendship. What a wonderful blessing occurs when your mate becomes your very best friend!

❷ The expression of **_eros_ love, which means _romance_**.

While the actual word *eros* is not found in the Bible, certainly the meaning or the picture of the word is found in God's Word. Take a moment to read the Song of Solomon 2:1-5. Notice the expressions of romance such as, "…His banner over me was love" (2:4), "…I am sick {overwhelmed} of love" (2:5). Wise couples, regardless of age or health, keep romance alive in their marriage.

❸ The expression of **_storge_ love, which means _security, trust_**.

As is true of *eros*, while the word *storge* is not found in the Bible, clearly the meaning is seen in Song of Solomon 2:8-14. The *storge* aspect of love is not fancy nor flashy. It is a secure kind of love in that it fits just right and surely is comfortable.

Notice how the lover appears in places that would be off-limits to anyone else. But because of the *storge* love, the "we-belong-together" kind of fit and security, he appears at the windows and lattice (2:9), and then again in the secret places of the stairs (2:14). This takes place in a perfectly comfortable setting because of the growing security and trust of the *storge* love.

❹ The expression of **_epithumeo_ love, which means _passion_**.

This word found in the New Testament is usually used in the negative sense of lust. In Philippians 1:23, however, Paul uses it as a passionate desire when he cries, "For I am in a strait betwixt two, having a *desire* to depart, and to be with Christ; which is far better." This desire is *epithumeo*, which is a strong passion or a deep craving.

When used in the framework of marriage, it is the strong attraction to your mate. It is found in the most intimate expression of sexual connection as husband and wife. This intimacy is never shared with another as long as life lasts.

❺ The expression of **_agape_ love, which means _unconditional commitment_**.

This is the most familiar type of love to the believer. The New Testament concept of this love is expressed even when it is not deserved or returned. In 1 John 4:7-11, the Apostle expresses the depth and beauty of *agape* love.

You will demonstrate your love for your mate through becoming best friends, keeping romance alive in your marriage, developing a strong sense of security and trust, making sure your passion is directed solely toward your mate, and loving your partner unconditionally. These are the five ways love is communicated and connection is experienced.

> This is the most familiar type of love to the believer. The New Testament concept of this love is expressed even when it is not deserved or returned. In 1 John 4:7-11, the Apostle expresses the depth and beauty of *agape* love.

> **Optional Teaching Point—Pause the DVD.**
> Perhaps these terms are new to many of the couples viewing the DVD. This is a good opportunity to review these five pictures and bring additional teaching to this moment. The couples may wish to ask questions about these terms as well as how to apply them. They will be working on these in their homework section.
> **After the discussion, resume the DVD.**

Practical ways to demonstrate all five kinds of love

The five expressions of love are wonderful blessings. For your mate to understand your expression of love, however, you must communicate it by the following eight demonstrations.

❶ The way you reach out to your mate with **touches of endearment**.

❷ The **words of value and worth** you select to communicate with your mate.

❸ The **little things you give or make** that assure your mate that he or she is on your mind.

❹ The **actions of thoughtfulness** that tell your mate it is a joy to encourage you. Thoughtful actions consistently demonstrated are such an encouragement in marriage.

❺ The **moments you share together** will communicate the importance and significance your sweetheart holds in your life.

❻ The specific **things you do to bless each other** are encouragements that occur beyond the normal anticipated actions. They are the little surprises and unanticipated joys that come because of your love for Christ and for your mate that encourages your partner spiritually.

❼ The **memories you make together** in shared activities, secrets communicated, and little things that have significance to you and your mate.

❽ The **reminders of your love** will be those things truly unique to you and your mate. These come in the form of little notes, cards, things that are said, and little actions that affirm, "I love you."

These practical demonstrations express your love and devotion. Consistently practiced, these actions really do build marriages.

The description of what might happen

Instead of growing closer together, some couples actually drift apart by building walls that divide and separate them. While there are many ways couples push each other apart, it is important to see the seven walls couples commonly experience.

> Ask the couples to share their own expectations, i.e., before they married. Were some unrealistic? Too high? Naive?

Note: As the leader, you are welcome to add notes for additional comments on any of these areas.

❶ **Expectations** that are not realized. An expectation is how you think your mate will act and what the situation is going to be. Here are several actual expectations expressed to Dr. Peck in counseling:

Lady: "I expect my husband is not only going to love me but is going to be romantic every single day."

Man: "I expect my wife is going to cook the same way my mother does."

Lady: "I expect my husband is going to appreciate all my efforts and is going to tell me how special I am every day."

Man: "I expect my wife is going to be ready for intimacy as soon as I suggest it."

Lady: "I expect my husband is going to tell me the details of his day. When he gets home from work, he is going to enjoy talking with me about everything."

Man: "I expect my wife will understand when I get home I just want a little quietness without talking all night long."

❷ **Promises** that are not fulfilled. There are times when emergencies occur and plans may change quickly. But when promises are consistently broken, serious walls are erected.

❸ **Conflicts** that are not resolved continue to build barriers that hurt connection.

④ **Schedules** that are not wisely managed frequently result in little or no time for you and your mate to communicate, make memories, or invest time with the Lord.

⑤ **Actions** that are not thoughtful quickly push partners apart.

⑥ **Communication** that is lacking hinders the joy of closeness.

⑦ **Experiences** that are not shared result in isolation and a coldness.

Be watching for opportunities that will bring you closer and give you a better connection in your marriage. Find ways to build bridges to your mate. Be on guard and on high alert for those things that could hinder or damage your relationship by creating a wall between you and your mate.

Every day you will be building either a bridge or a wall. Bridges make connection possible. Walls destroy this wonderful connection by erecting barriers that keep couples apart. By the grace of God, determine that you will be a builder of bridges.

DVD concludes

Make the most of this moment

The pictures of bridges and walls are vivid images that will open the door for significant teaching to conclude this session. The closing moments of this presentation lend themselves well to presenting the Gospel (Christ *bridged* the gap between God and the sinner and tore down a great *wall* of sin that separated us from God). Believing couples may be challenged to begin viewing their marriage from the picture of the bridge or the wall.

Encourage the couples to invest time together this week. They will be working on communicating genuine love and detecting barriers they may not even know exist. Be much in prayer for your couples as this week will be potentially significant in their connecting with each other and developing closeness on the journey of a lifetime.

> The pictures of bridges and walls are vivid images that will open the door for significant teaching to conclude this session. The closing moments of this presentation lend themselves well to presenting the Gospel (Christ *bridged* the gap between God and the sinner and tore down a great *wall* of sin that separated us from God).

Let's work on connecting this week

As the leader it is important for you to know exactly what the couple will be working on at home. It is wise for you to read through the *Couple's Edition* and complete the homework for two reasons. First, it will help you prepare for the introduction to the next session. Second, it may help and strengthen your own marriage as well. The following is the material as it is presented in their *Couple's Edition*.

During the next several days, you will have several special assignments to complete both individually and together. These assignments are designed to help you to think honestly about your marriage. It is possible that in the "busyness" of your lives, the demands of your schedules, and the responsibilities of raising children, your marriage may need some extra attention. The homework this week will focus on the significance of genuine love and how it is communicated as well as how to detect major walls that need to be removed.

Read again the story of Mark and Samantha and answer the following questions in your own words.

❶ What were some of the major walls that were building up in their marriage?

_____
_____
_____
_____
_____
_____
_____

❷ What did the Lord use to finally break through to Mark and Samantha?

_____
_____
_____
_____
_____
_____
_____

❸ How does the story of Mark and Samantha compare with your marriage?

___ Absolutely nothing at all; we have nothing in common.

___ At times we share a little in common with them.

___ Often we face similar situations.

___ Mark and Samantha could easily be us. We share much in common with them.

❹ Review these five descriptions of love.
- *Phileo* is the kind of love that is expressed as *being good friends*.
- *Eros* is the special kind of love that is *romantic*.
- *Storge* is the kind of love that senses that you really *fit together well*. It produces security and trust.
- *Epithumeo* is passion and is expressed with a *very strong desire for your mate*.
- *Agape* is the *unconditional love* that is committed to seeking the well-being of your mate even if it is not deserved or returned.

Write a brief paragraph in your own guide answering the questions.

❺ How am I demonstrating these five loves to my mate? Are there areas in which I can improve?

_____
_____
_____
_____
_____
_____
_____
_____

❻ How is your mate demonstrating these five loves to you? Are there areas in which you would like your mate to improve?

_____
_____
_____
_____
_____
_____
_____

❼ Take time to carefully read through and think about the eight ways in which these five loves are expressed. Think about your marriage as you consider this important material.

The Lord has wonderfully built within us not only the need to be loved and the capability to love others but also the ability to show it! If connecting is ever to take place in your marriage, you must consistently demonstrate it in a way that your mate understands and appreciates. The key to this is communicating in the way that means the most to your marriage partner. What does he or she appreciate and perceive as a loving communication?

The **touches of endearment** are the tender times that you reach out and physically connect with your sweetheart. It may include a lingering kiss or a tender hug. When you are walking with your mate, do you hold his or her hand? Don't walk ahead by five or ten paces. Walk with your mate and physically connect with him or her.

Words that communicate value and worth are statements that affirm your love and thankfulness for your partner. You may speak these words to your mate or write them in little notes that you leave for your partner to discover. It comes to your partner in the form of affirming not only what he or she does but also who your partner is and is becoming.

Giving little love-gifts or making something for your mate are expressions that show that your partner is on your mind and heart. It is the thoughtful little gift you know your partner really appreciates or the craft you make that communicates your mate's significance. The key to this is giving what your mate really enjoys—not necessarily what *you* like!

Thoughtful actions are those little surprises you find joy in doing because they are special to your mate. A wide range of possibilities include doing chores around the house, watching a sporting event your mate enjoys, preparing something special for your partner, or helping with something that will invest in your mate's life and your relationship.

Busy couples often discover that it is becoming increasingly difficult to **find moments shared together**, and yet they are so cherished. These are the moments when couples enjoy sitting together, holding hands, and discovering the joy of being together. For those couples who have been blessed with children, these moments may be a little more challenging to find, but benefits of doing so are tremendous.

Finding creative ways to bless each other builds on the thoughtful actions. The blessing comes both from encouraging your mate's spiritual life as well as from sharing little surprises that result in joy for your part-

> If connecting is ever to take place in your marriage, you must consistently demonstrate it in a way that your mate understands and appreciates. The key to this is communicating in the way that means the most to your marriage partner. What does he or she appreciate and perceive as a loving communication?

ner. Doing only what is expected is important; but it may not be special. Going beyond the expected communicates how special your mate is and how much you treasure your marriage.

Making memories that will last a lifetime does not require lots of money or even time. These memories are built in the times shared together and importance you attach to your marriage. You can make precious memories in the special times you share in devotions or in the meaningful conversations that take place on the front porch or even in the quiet times around the campfire, or in secrets you share with no one else.

We make memories by taking a walk after supper and reminding your mate how special he or she is to you. This is a memory that warms the heart of your mate for a long time. It is the dreams you share, the funny things that happen, as well as how you held each other in the hard times that will make memories on your journey.

You **demonstrate the reminders of your love** by remembering to observe the mile-markers such as birthdates and anniversaries. It is remembering and talking about the little things that are special only to you and your mate. You establish the reminders of your love through sharing things known only to you as a married couple. It is the frequent assurance that your mate is significant; it is the precious joy you share because you belong to each other and to no other. These are the great reminders of your love.

After reading through this list once again, select a time that is convenient for both of you to talk about the items that mean the most to each other. If you aren't sure which items on the list are more significant to your mate, ask him or her. Make this a special time. Commit to doing better at demonstrating your love.

As you have thoughtfully considered this list, perhaps a few thoughts have come to your mind. Now is a good time to write down several things that require both prayer and attention.

_____

_____

_____

_____

_____

_____

After you have talked through this, take a few moments to read 1 John 4:7-21 and be sure to pray together.

❽ Read through this list of things that erect walls in marriages.
- Expectations not realized
- Promises not fulfilled
- Conflicts not resolved
- Schedules not wisely managed
- Actions not thoughtful or careful
- Communication that is lacking
- Experiences not shared

Are you aware of any of these walls in your marriage? If yes, which ones?

_____
_____
_____
_____
_____
_____
_____

> When you talk with your partner about the way love is being expressed in your marriage, it will be important to talk about the walls. Sometimes one partner is aware of a wall that the other partner does not yet see. Be careful not to assign blame or become argumentative.

When you talk with your partner about the way love is being expressed in your marriage, it will be important to talk about the walls. Sometimes one partner is aware of a wall that the other partner does not yet see. Be careful not to assign blame or become argumentative. Talk quietly and heed the strong command of Ephesians 4:15: "But speaking the truth in love, may grow up into him in all things, which is the head, even Christ."

Before the next DVD session, be sure to read the story of Gene and Alyssa in chapter 4.

Additional things the Lord is teaching me

_____
_____
_____

Chapter 4—Wise Ways to Build Bridges

One Word You Will Never Forget in Marriage-Building!

Every day provides me with the opportunity to lovingly reach out to my mate with a bridge, or to carelessly push my mate away with a wall. Walls are important in prisons, but devastating in marriages.

"He brought me to the banqueting house, and His banner over me was love."
(Song of Solomon 2:4)

Before you present the DVD

Your couples return for the fourth step in building closeness. Some may be discovering how distant they have become with their partner. Perhaps some of these couples will need to make an appointment with you to discuss their marriage situation. You will have the opportunity to personally invest in their marriage.

Hopefully all of your couples are serious about completing their homework. These assignments are designed to help them grow in their fellowship with Christ and their relationship with each other. This will take place as they learn to better communicate, invest time with the Lord through Bible reading and prayer, and find enjoyment being together.

Preview the DVD

Once again you will determine whether to show the entire DVD or select the **Optional conclusion**. As you preview the DVD, note the points you want to stress in the margins. It is helpful to read through the *Couple's Edition* to see how their material correlates with your *Leader's Edition* as well as to know ahead of time what their homework will be.

> Your couples return for the fourth step in building closeness. Some may be discovering how distant they have become with their partner. Perhaps some of these couples will need to make an appointment with you to discuss their marriage situation.

Goals to consider

While every setting will offer unique challenges and opportunities, you should keep in mind several goals for this session:

❶ *Continue to encourage your couples to visualize the picture of bridges and walls.* Help them to understand the blessing of building a bridge as well as seeing the danger of carelessly and thoughtlessly building a wall. Bridges connect. Walls separate.

❷ *Prepare a strategy to help the couples to be intentional in their bridge-building.* One way to help them is to review the eight ways genuine love is broadcast as well as the seven ways walls are built from the previous session.

❸ *Take a few moments to reflect upon your own marriage.* As the leader, you have the great opportunity of genuinely practicing what you are encouraging your couples to do. Would your mate say there are more bridges or walls in your own marriage?

The couples will meet and think about Gene and Alyssa

(Your couples should have read this story before coming to the session.)

> Gene and Alyssa are typical of the couples in their neighborhood. They both have professional jobs that require separate commutes. They never attend church, except for Alyssa's uncle's funeral and an occasional friend's wedding. They devote their weekends to working around the house, going to the bar on Saturday night, and sleeping in on Sunday morning.
>
> Around their sixth wedding anniversary, things began to change in their home. Gene began to ask questions about God, the Bible, and even church. A friend at work took great interest in Gene and invited him to attend the before-work Bible study in their department. Reluctantly, Gene went to one of the early morning fellowships. The men and women in the Bible study were studying and discussing the book of Ephesians. While Gene was very nervous that first day, he was also very struck with the amazing truth he heard. Throughout the day, he could not get over the thought, "For by grace are ye saved through faith: and that not of yourselves: it is the gift of God: Not of works, lest any man should boast" (Ephesians 2:8-9). He could not wait to get home and tell Alyssa.
>
> Her response was far from what Gene had hoped it would be. In a harsh tone she said, "What are you, crazy? I don't think it is a good idea for you to spend any more time around those cultists."

Continue to encourage your couples to visualize the picture of bridges and walls. Help them to understand the blessing of building a bridge as well as seeing the danger of carelessly and thoughtlessly building a wall. Bridges connect. Walls separate.

"They most certainly are not cultists," Gene replied quietly as he eased onto the couch. He leaned forward and looked into his wife's eyes and said, "I think they have the answer to what is missing in my life, Alyssa. I have filled my life with things and pleasures. But I have never given any thought to God, or the Bible, or what is going to happen to me when I die."

"Oh, *great*—now my husband is getting religion. Well, honey, if that is what you want, I won't stop you. But just don't expect me to have anything to do with this nonsense," Alyssa told him with a sarcastic tone.

Several weeks later after one of the early morning Bible studies, Gene placed his faith in Christ. His manager happily pointed Gene to God's plan of salvation by taking him to several verses in the Book of Romans. Gene was thrilled because he knew for sure then that he belonged to the Lord. How desperately he wanted Alyssa to know the same joy!

His dear Alyssa continued to insist that she wanted nothing to do with this "religion business." Though Gene assured her that it was not a religion, but rather a relationship with Christ, she adamantly resisted. Gene was changing. He no longer wanted to go to the bar. He now wanted to get up for church. He was more thoughtful and helpful around the house. Alyssa liked *that* part of the new Gene, but she resented the fact that he claimed to know God and where he would go when he died. She didn't have that assurance, and instead of asking Gene what it meant, she resisted and built walls in their marriage.

Several years later, Alyssa was transferred to another branch of the bank where she worked. Though all the customers would be new and she would have a lot to learn, the new branch was closer to her home and she was happy for the opportunity.

Shortly after Alyssa began work at the new branch, an older couple came into the bank. They were talking quietly and holding hands as they approached Alyssa's counter. How pleasant this couple was and, obviously, how deeply in love they were! As Alyssa efficiently took care of their banking, she overheard Richard whisper "I love you" to his wife, Jeannette.

"That was sweet," Alyssa said quietly to the couple. "I hope my husband and I will love each other as much as you two do when we get to be your age," she added.

Without a second's hesitation, Richard told her, "Well, I can tell you it will be a lot more likely if you include the Lord in your relationship. My wife and I have been married for 57 years. Our first eight years were not so good. But then we came to know the Lord and have included Him in our lives ever since. Hasn't been perfect, but the Lord surely has changed our lives," Richard told her as he picked up his deposit slip.

Alyssa couldn't forget his statement: "It will be a lot more likely if you include the Lord." But she kept telling herself, "That's silly. They are just old people. Get over it." As hard as she tried, though, she knew it was the desire of her heart that she and her husband would be so in love at that stage of life.

That encounter got Alyssa thinking about just how empty her life really was. She had built a number of walls in her marriage. She knew Gene had something that she did not. The weight of her sin and guilt became overwhelming. Within several weeks, she could not wait another day. Alyssa asked Gene to show her how she, too, could know Christ.

For Gene and Alyssa, this was not the end of their story but only the beginning. To fulfill God's plan for marriage, couples must build their marriages upon Christ and build bridges to experience the great joy of connecting.

You may wish to review the story of Gene and Alyssa as a good way to introduce the DVD.

Presenting the DVD "Wise Ways to Build Bridges"

Typically, the couples will prepare for each DVD presentation by reading the introductory material. If some have not done so, briefly introduce the presentation by sharing the story of Gene and Alyssa.

At this time, open the session with prayer and share any other preliminary information. Remember that you can pause the DVD to share the **Optional teaching points.** You can also choose either to show the entire DVD (approximately 45 minutes) or to select the **Optional conclusion** at the 22-minute mark. These decision-points are clearly noted in your *Leader's Edition*.

<u>Note: The sections underlined in your leader's guide are blanks in the couple's guides to be filled in during the DVD.</u>

Introduce the DVD by reading the illustration of being on the journey

Remind the couples once again that every day each couple will be involved in a building project. Wise couples will intentionally reach out to each other by building bridges. Unwise couples will push each other apart by building walls. This is a good place for you to remind them of the truth presented in the opening of the chapter – *that walls are important in prisons but devastating in marriages.* After presenting the two pictures of bridges and walls, it is time to show the DVD.

> Remember that you can pause the DVD to share the **Optional teaching points.** You can also choose either to show the entire DVD (approximately 45 minutes) or to select the **Optional conclusion** at the 22-minute mark.

Start the DVD

Introduction

It is interesting to see how sometimes a simple word association can help us to remember. The third-grade teacher helped her class remember how to spell "arithmetic" with the silly statement "a rat in the house might eat the ice cream." At least one of her students never forgot that word association.

As they are encouraged to build bridges in their marriage, the couples will be introduced to a word they do not expect. While it may surprise some, and may sound silly to others, remembering this specific word and the six things the acrostic represents will help them build bridges and closeness in their marriage.

> Connecting through WAFFLES! When you think of the pursuit of being connected to your mate, keep in mind the word *WAFFLE*.

 Think of the pursuit, **be connected.**

When you think of the pursuit of being connected to your mate, keep in mind the word *WAFFLE*. In this case, waffle does not refer to a breakfast item nor to the act of changing of one's mind on an issue. It's better than either! Work through these six important things involved in building bridges, and closeness, by remembering the "WAFFLE." (Feel free to write additional notes in the space provided beside each of the statements.)

WAFFLE

W stands for **Wholly follow the Lord (1 Peter 2:21)**.

Christ left an example for us so that we might follow His steps. How do you follow the steps of the Lord? While it is not limited to just these activities, following the steps of the Lord certainly involves daily reading the Bible, investing time in prayer, actively worshiping, serving in your Bible-believing church, and having a devotional time with your mate. Wonderful blessings result when couples determine to "Wholly follow the Lord."

_____
_____
_____
_____
_____
_____

A stands for **Appreciation, affection and affirmation (Matthew 7:12)**.

Matthew 7:12 is part of a sermon the Lord Jesus preached. Specifically, this verse is often called the "golden rule." Here the Lord reminds his followers to treat others in the way they wish to be treated. "Appreciation, affection, and affirmation" are three very necessary ingredients in the building of strong bridges in marriages.

F stands for **Forgiveness (Ephesians 4:30-32)**.

Often forgiveness is associated with the cancellation of a major debt. Imagine how you would feel if your bank informed you that someone had paid off your mortgage and your debt had been forgiven! Likewise, there is joy in the godly marriage relationship when "Forgiveness" is both asked for and granted.

Optional Teaching Point—Pause the DVD.

Taking a few moments to explore the richness of the teaching of Ephesians 4:30-32 may prove to be well worth the investment. Consider with the couples this outline and the teaching of the Word.

- **The Possibility:** "And grieve not the Holy Spirit of God" (4:30a). Explore briefly the concept of the word *grieve.*
- **The Position:** "Whereby ye are sealed unto the day of redemption" (Ephesians 4:30b).
- **The Poison:** "Let all bitterness, and wrath, and anger, and clamour, and evil speaking, be put away from you, with all malice" (4:31). It is important for the couples to understand the danger of harbored anger. Note Ephesians 4:26.
- **The Purpose:** "And be ye kind one to another, tenderhearted, forgiving one another" (4:32a). It is interesting to note the anger issues of 4:31 are so unlike Christ, while the issues of grace in 4:32 are so like the Lord.
- **The Pattern:** "Even as God for Christ's sake hath forgiven you" (4:32b). As the Father has forgiven you, for the sake of Christ, you can forgive others for the sake of the Lord through his power.

After the discussion, resume the DVD.

F stands for <u>**Fellowship (1 John 1:3-6)**</u>.

The New Testament word for fellowship is *koinonia*, which means "that which you share in common with another." It is the sharing together of life experiences with the Lord as well with your mate. This idea of "Fellowship" cannot function very well when walls are erected.

_____
_____
_____
_____
_____
_____
_____

L stands for <u>**Love that is expressed consistently (Romans 5:8)**</u>.

God's love is consistently expressed to us through His Word, the Bible, and He has demonstrated it by His actions. How incredible was our Lord's sacrifice as He took our sin upon Himself and experienced the wrath of His holy Father. Likewise, wise couples not only express their love but they also *demonstrate* it.

_____
_____
_____
_____
_____
_____
_____

E stands for **Example of trust and devotion.**

Proverbs 5:18-19 reveals the love and devotion a husband is to express. He is to live in such a way as to communicate to his wife that she is the source of his joy and satisfaction. Husbands, this is practical and powerful in building a bridge to your wife.

> **Proverbs 5:18-19** reveals the love and devotion a husband is to express.
> **Proverbs 31:1** reveals the love and devotion a wife is to express.

_____
_____
_____
_____
_____
_____

Proverbs 31:11 reveals the love and devotion a wife is to express. The wife is to live in such a way that the heart of her husband will fully trust in her. He does not worry about what she is doing, what she is saying, or what she is spending. Wives, this is practical and powerful in building a bridge to your husband.

_____

4: Wise Ways to Build Bridges – 67

_____
_____
_____
_____
_____
_____
_____
_____

> **Optional Conclusion—You may stop the DVD here.**
>
> Wise couples understand that marriages either grow closer, and deeper in connection by building bridges, or they will slowly drift apart because of walls. In the next session of viewing the DVD "Wise Ways to Build Bridges", we will examine how trust and devotion as demonstrated by husbands in Proverbs 5:18-19, and by wives in Proverbs 31:11.
>
> This week, take seriously the pictures of bridges and walls. Ask yourself, "Is this action a bridge or a wall?" Learn to be sensitive to these situations. Seek the Lord's help to build bridges and tear down walls.
>
> **
>
> If you choose this **Optional conclusion** then begin the next viewing of the DVD "Wise Ways to Build Bridges" with the following material:
>
> - Review the marriage of Gene and Alyssa.
> - Remind the couples that closeness throughout their marriage is made possible by the Lord.
> - Rehearse with the couples the word "WAFFLE" and list the six statements to begin this session.
>
> **Open with prayer and begin the DVD.**

How are you and your mate doing with the "waffle"? It is important to remember that marriage bridges are constructed not of bricks and iron but rather by consistently applying these six important principles.

❷ Think of the partnership, **be lovingly committed**.

Turn to Ephesians 5:21-27. How will you express the principles of "waffle" to each other? For true connection to occur you must embrace these principles as true and express them in action. You will find it is not enough to simply believe these principles. Commit to what the Lord says and take the next step and express these principles in action.

The commitment of the wise couple (5:21):

Successful marriages are never built upon selfishness and the demand to have one's own way. A selfish person often thinks the universe revolves around him or her. Wise marriages are built upon submitting to one another and making each other the higher priority.

The commitment of the wise wife (5:22-24):

As the church loves and respects Christ, so the wise wife honors, loves, and respects both her husband himself and the office he holds. From a military perspective, *submission* refers to lining up the troops. In non-military terms, it means a voluntary decision to respect your husband and willingly line up with him. If your husband lives in such a way that you cannot respect him personally, you still must respect the God-appointed office he holds as your husband.

The commitment of the wise husband (5:25-27):

Notice how high and awesome are the standards to which the Lord holds husbands as spiritual leaders. You, as the husband, are admonished to love your wife *even as Christ loved you.* As Christ gave Himself for His church, you are to give yourself to and for your wife.

> **Optional Teaching Point—Pause the DVD.**
>
> Taking a few moments to explore the richness of the teaching of Ephesians 5:21-27 may prove to be well worth the investment. With your couples, study the text and explore more deeply the love and respect wives must give to their husbands. Take time to walk step by step through the text how husbands are to function based on the way Christ relates to the church.
>
> **After the discussion, resume the DVD.**

These special bridge-building exercises are not hardships. They are great opportunities to build closeness with Him and your mate.

DVD concludes

Make the most of this moment

The couples have been brought face-to-face with the six important bridge-building principles for enjoying fellowship with the Lord and a great relationship with each other. Wise wives communicate respect and appreciation to their husbands. Wise husbands communicate that they love and cherish their wives. Seize this moment to build into your couples another important principle the Lord Jesus taught. It is found in John 13:17: "If ye know these things, happy are ye if ye do them."

This may be the perfect time to specifically challenge your couples to make a spiritual decision. Are you sure each participant really knows the Lord personally? Or are there some in your group that really need to hear the Gospel once again? Are there couples who have become careless in their marriage and the walls are obvious? A special time of invitation may well be in order.

Encourage the couples to take seriously their homework this week. The homework this week focuses on the joy of living for Christ and living for each other.

Let's work on connecting this week

As the leader it is important for you to know exactly what the couple will be working on at home. It is wise for you to read through the *Couple's Edition* and complete the homework for two reasons. First, it will help you prepare for the introduction to the next session. Second, it may help and strengthen your own marriage as well. The following is the material as it is presented in their *Couple's Edition*.

During the next several days, you will have several special assignments to complete both individually and together as a couple. These assignments are designed to help you to think honestly about your marriage and your walk with the Lord. If you are like many couples, you know how full your schedule has become. Please remember that the time you invest on completing your homework will reap benefits that will last not only for your lifetime but will pave the way for the next generation to live godly lives as well.

Think about the state of your spiritual life. You and your partner will work on the following questions separately. When both of you are finished with the assignment, compare your answers. If you don't understand your mate's answer, or if you have questions, be careful not to become argumentative. These few questions will provide a wonderful opportunity for you and your mate to talk, pray, and better connect on the journey of a lifetime.

Before you begin to answer these questions, ask the Lord to help you to be honest both with yourself and with your mate. This may be the time the Lord greatly desires to bless your life and help you to grow as a believer. For this to happen, you must be totally honest in your evaluation.

> As the leader it is important for you to know exactly what the couple will be working on at home. It is wise for you to read through the *Couple's Edition* and complete the homework for two reasons. First, it will help you prepare for the introduction to the next session. Second, it may help and strengthen your own marriage as well. The following is the material as it is presented in their *Couple's Edition*.

Please answer these questions using a scale of 1 to 4.

    1 = Very strongly disagree, as this almost never describes my situation.
    2 = Mildly disagree, as this usually does not describe my situation.
    3 = Mildly agree, as this sometimes describes my situation.
    4 = Strongly agree, as this usually describes my situation.

❶ **The spiritual climate of our marriage and home** (Use the scale of 1-4 to answer.)

    ___ 1. I know the Lord as my personal Savior and seek to live for the Lord Jesus.
    ___ 2. I want to know and do the will of God. The will of God is a great priority in my life.
    ___ 3. I read the Bible nearly every day.
    ___ 4. I am a member of a Bible-believing church.
    ___ 5. I serve in a regular ministry in my church.
    ___ 6. I can honestly say that my mate and I agree on the importance of living for Christ and that both of us are seeking to live for Him.
    ___ 7. I have witnessed my mate reading the Bible, praying, and serving in some area of Christian service in our local church.
    ___ 8. I am encouraged that my mate is consistent in praying with me on a regular basis.
    ___ 9. I can honestly say that my mate and I talk regularly about spiritual matters.
    ___10. I know that my mate is growing spiritually and is becoming a mature disciple of the Lord Jesus Christ.

❷ **How I view things relating to my home and marriage** (Use the scale of 1-4 to answer.)

    ___ 1. My mate and I have a strong relationship of trust and mutual respect.
    ___ 2. My mate and I talk about finances and budgeting and are in agreement with how our finances are handled.
    ___ 3. My mate and I talk about the things that make a marriage strong. We are seeking to implement these things in our marriage.
    ___ 4. My mate has a good relationship with his or her parents.
    ___ 5. I have a good relationship with my parents.
    ___ 6. My mate and I talk about parenting and how we are raising our children.
    ___ 7. My mate and I are satisfied with the present level of our communication with each other.

___ 8. My mate and I are pleased with the amount of time we have to spend together.

___ 9. My mate and I can readily detect the love we share and how it is demonstrated by building bridges.

___ 10. My mate and I do not know of any walls that are keeping us apart.

❸ **My personal spiritual condition** (Simply check the answers that apply to you.)

___ I know the Lord as Savior.
___ I sometimes doubt my salvation.
___ I struggle with the assurance of salvation.
___ I am growing in my spiritual life.
___ I read the Bible nearly every day.
___ I pray throughout the day.
___ I am certain that my mate knows the Lord as personal Savior.
___ I grew up in a Christian home.
___ I am the first Christian in my family.
___ I regularly pray with my mate.
___ I am a member of a Bible-believing church.
___ I am faithful in attendance at my local church.
___ I enjoying serving in our local church.
___ I can honestly say that the Lord has first priority in my life.

When you and your mate are finished answering these questions, find a good time to sit down and talk through each answer.

List several strong points in your spiritual life and marriage that you are thankful for:

_____
_____
_____
_____
_____
_____
_____

List several weak points that you have detected in your spiritual life and marriage?

_____
_____
_____
_____
_____
_____
_____

Together as husband and wife ask the Lord to work in the areas that need improvement. If you and your mate know how to strengthen the weak areas, commit to each other that you will begin to build bridges *immediately*. If you do not know how to correct a faulty area, make an appointment with your pastor. *Do not procrastinate.*

❹ Make the reading of God's Word a high priority this week. The Bible is your source of spiritual nourishment. Do not starve spiritually! If you are not in the habit of reading the Bible daily, a good place to start is the Gospel of John. Each chapter reveals something wonderful about the Son of God, the Lord Jesus Christ.

❺ Intentionally build a bridge to your mate every day by being thoughtful and affectionate and demonstrating your appreciation. Ask yourself each day, "How can I deliberately build a bridge to my sweetheart by something I do or say?" Ask yourself each night at bedtime, "Have I built a wall or a bridge today?" If you identify any walls, at a mutually convenient time, talk with your mate and begin to take steps to remove them.

> If you are not in the habit of intentionally building bridges, take a few moments at the start of each day to write down two or three words to say and actions you will take to build bridges. At bedtime, check your list and ask yourself: *Did I actually build any bridges today?*

If you are not in the habit of intentionally building bridges, take a few moments at the start of each day to write down two or three words to say and actions you will take to build bridges. At bedtime, check your list and ask yourself: *Did I actually build any bridges today?*

Tearing down walls is often a process – *not* a single action. Make a list of two or three things you can do to chip away at the wall each day. Be gentle. Be thoughtful. Be much in prayer as you seek the Lord's guidance and blessing.

Your living proclamation

Make this little proclamation a very real part of your life and marriage.

*Father, You have brought me into a wonderful fellowship
with You through the Lord Jesus.*

How great is Your grace and mercy.

I deserve nothing.

Everything I have is from Your amazing hand.

*May my fellowship be sweet
as I learn to wholly follow You.*

*May I learn to freely share my
appreciation, affection, and affirmation
with my beloved mate.*

May I forgive as You forgive me.

May my love be as clearly expressed as Your love for me.

*May my devotion and trust be guarded
carefully and joyfully.*

Lord, to do this, I need You.

I want You.

I depend upon You.

*I will not excuse myself by saying,
"I am only human."*

For with You, all things are possible.

*Lord, together, let's build bridges in my marriage
on this journey of a lifetime.*

Before the next DVD session, be sure to read the story of Timothy and Elizabeth in chapter 5.

Additional things the Lord is teaching me

_____

_____

_____

_____

_____

_____

Chapter 5—What Makes Closeness Possible?

Sweetheart, You are Special to Me!

When someone holds the title of being special, never treat that person as common or ordinary. Did I demonstrate and communicate today just how special my mate, my lover, and my best friend really is to me?

*"...Let my beloved come into his garden,
and eat his pleasant fruits."
(Song of Solomon 4:16)*

Before you present the DVD

Your couples return for the fifth step in building closeness. Song of Solomon 4:16 compares joyful intimacy, generously shared with your beloved mate, to "eating his pleasant fruits." Some couples have discovered how lacking they are in intimacy. One reason for the lack of closeness in marriage may be the absence of communicating how special the mate really is. Perhaps there is a couple in the group who needs to make an appointment with you to discuss their marital situation. If so, you will have the opportunity to personally invest in their marriage.

Hopefully all of your couples are serious in completing their homework. These assignments are designed to help them grow in their fellowship with Christ and in their relationship with each other. This will take place as they learn to better communicate, invest time with the Lord through Bible reading and prayer, and enjoy being together.

Preview the DVD

Once again you will determine whether to show the entire DVD or select the **Optional conclusion**. As you preview the DVD, note the points you want to stress in the margins. It is helpful to read through the *Couple's Edition* to see how their material correlates with your *Leader's Edition* as well as to know ahead of time what their homework will be.

> Your couples return for the fifth step in building closeness. **Song of Solomon 4:16** compares joyful intimacy, generously shared with your beloved mate, to "eating his pleasant fruits." Some couples have discovered how lacking they are in intimacy. One reason for the lack of closeness in marriage may be the absence of communicating how special the mate really is.

Goals to consider

While every setting will offer unique challenges and opportunities, you should keep in mind several goals for this session:

❶ *Seek to create vivid, easy-to-remember word pictures with the images of a beautiful lawn (and its opposite) and a healthy bank account (and its opposite).*

❷ *Help the couples to see that "Sweetheart, You are Special to Me!" is more than the title of this session. Rather, it is the precious demonstration and communication of two married people who are growing in connection.*

❸ *Use the story of Timothy and Elizabeth to challenge and encourage your couples.* Grandpa and Grandma did not *accidentally* arrive at connection and closeness in their marriage. At 61 years of marriage, this dear couple was intentional in developing closeness. The grandson and his future mate were so wise to determine to learn from those who really did love each other on the journey of a lifetime!

They made the spiritual decisions to trust the Lord, walk daily with God through the Word and prayer, view their marriage as a covenant, never take each other for granted, and never go to bed mad at each other. This should be stressed in this session.

> Do you know an elderly couple who are vibrant and growing in their love for the Lord and for each other? If so, consider having them give a brief testimony before you show the DVD.

Do you know an elderly couple who are vibrant and growing in their love for the Lord and for each other? If so, consider having them give a brief testimony before you show the DVD. (It may be wise to ask them to write out their testimony. You may need to help them with the wording.)

The couples will meet and think about Timothy and Elizabeth

(Your couples should have read this story before coming to the session.)

> Timothy and Elizabeth often referred to themselves as "simple folk who learned to trust the Lord and love each other." Those who knew them would dispute the word "simple." But there was no denying how much they trusted the Lord and loved each other.
>
> Timothy and Elizabeth were teenagers the night they met at a special service under the big tent hosted by several Bible-believing churches in their Midwestern town. One evening the evangelist gave an invitation. He said, "Those who really want to live for the Lord, and put Him first in their lives, come forward as we sing the closing hymn. Take your stand, and make it public as we sing."
>
> Timothy came from the left aisle, and Elizabeth came from the right aisle. Each was convinced that Christ must be first in all

aspects of life. In his message earlier in the evening, the speaker had referred to this as "giving Christ the preeminence." Though neither knew exactly what that would entail, both knew that the Lord deserved nothing less than first place.

After prayer and counsel, the people who responded were dismissed. As Elizabeth turned to leave, she came face-to-face with Timothy. Elizabeth excused herself in this somewhat embarrassing and awkward situation and darted to the left. Timothy quickly extended his hand and said, "Tim's my name. Who are you? We both came forward."

At that point both burst out laughing as Elizabeth looked around and said, "Yes, indeed, we both came forward." That simple introduction grew into a friendship, which became a courtship, and then a beautiful June wedding three years later.

Timothy always rejoiced in the fact that he put the Lord first and met his sweetheart who was doing the same thing. They had no premarital counseling course. What they did have, however, was the example of both sets of parents who overcame obstacles, endured hardships, and not only put the Lord first in their lives but loved their mates.

A large family would bless their lives. Family times that centered on the reading of God's Word and prayer were some of the best times of the day. Not only did their family read the Word, but the entire family sought to apply God's Word to their daily living.

Now after the birth of many grandchildren, and even several great-grandchildren, Timothy's namesake came over to Grandpa and Grandma's house one night to tell them something very special. He could hardly contain himself as he told them the news.

"Grandpa, you know I was named after *you*?" Timothy said rather enthusiastically.

"Yep! I was just outside the door when you were born," Grandpa said with equal enthusiasm.

Timothy continued. "Well, you won't believe it. Grandma, I met a girl—well, a young lady—whose name is Elizabeth. She is going to the College and Career activity at our church with me this Friday. She is really something! Wouldn't it be something if this worked, and there was another Timothy and Elizabeth in the family?"

Both grandparents assured Timothy that it would indeed be wonderful *if* that was what the Lord had planned. Additionally, they encouraged him to move slowly and to really determine the Lord's will. Both assured Timothy of their love and prayers.

Before long he was on his way. His grandparents stood at the door and watched their grandson run down to his car. "Wouldn't that be something, Beth? Wouldn't that just be something?" the elder Timothy said as he put his arm around his dear wife's waist and hugged her.

> It was something indeed. The young couple dated, and it was a joy to watch their love and commitment grow. Both had a heart for the Lord and were eager to learn. Nearly 16 months later, the young Timothy and Elizabeth made a special appointment with the older Timothy and Elizabeth.
>
> "Grandpa and Grandma, we want our marriage to be like yours. We share the same names," Timothy said. "We also want to share the same secrets of how you made it to this point." Everyone laughed because Tim's statement didn't sound quite right. Quickly, Grandpa assured them that he understood exactly what young Timothy meant. They spent several wonderful evenings together as the grandparents rehearsed the spiritual decisions they had made, trusting the Lord, walking daily with God through the Word and prayer, viewing their marriage as a covenant, never taking each other for granted, as well as never going to bed mad at each other.
>
> How wonderful to build such a marriage that others can see and want to follow that pattern! Likewise, how special it is to find such a couple who has a heart to learn and a desire to improve.

You may wish to review the story of Timothy and Elizabeth as a good way to introduce the DVD.

Presenting the DVD "What Makes Closeness Possible?"

At this time, open the session with prayer and share any other preliminary information. Remember that you can pause the DVD to share the **Optional teaching points.** You can also choose either to show the entire DVD (approximately 40 minutes) or to select the **Optional conclusion** at the 20-minute mark. These decision-points are clearly noted in your *Leader's Edition*.

<u>Note: The sections that are underlined in your leader's guide are blanks in the couple's guide to be filled in during the DVD.</u>

Introduce the DVD with the illustration of the lawn and bank

Remind the couples once again that, every day, each couple will be involved in a building project. Wise couples *intentionally* reach out to each other in ways that demonstrate that their sweetheart is special. Two great word pictures that will help couples grasp the picture of a successful marriage are the lawn and the bank account.

Think about your lawn. What would happen if you never fertilized, mowed, trimmed, and watered your lawn? It would not take long for the signs of neglect to show up. Beautiful lawns do not just happen. They require attention, care, and nurturing. Likewise, beautiful marriages do not just happen. While there are no

---

Remember that you can pause the DVD to share the **Optional teaching points.** You can also choose either to show the entire DVD (approximately 40 minutes) or to select the **Optional conclusion** at the 20-minute mark.

perfect marriages, the results of trusting the Lord, applying biblical principles, and caring for each other in a loving way will result in beauty as the years go by.

Think about your bank account. Healthy bank accounts require more deposits than withdrawals. While this principle is very simple, healthy bank accounts demand it. Likewise, healthy marriages that stay beautiful through the years are those in which the couples carefully and deliberately make more deposits than withdrawals.

Thoughtful actions, loving words, and specific things that communicate affection and appreciation are deposits. Thoughtless acts, unresolved conflicts, and broken promises are serious withdrawals. When deposits become the norm and withdrawals the rare exception, healthy marriages grow as the couples make each other special.

Song of Solomon Chapter 2: Closeness

Turn to Song of Solomon chapter 2. In the final session, notice several things that are very significant in making closeness special.

Looks through special eyes 2:1-7

Remember the culture and context in which this text was written. It is important to see how the bride and bridegroom view each other.

The bride speaks in verse 1: *"I am the rose of Sharon, and the lily of the valleys."* These are wild flowers that are very common in Israel. The bride views herself as very ordinary and common.

The bridegroom speaks in verse 2: *"As the lily among thorns, so is my love among the daughters."* The bridegroom views his beloved through special eyes and communicates that there is nothing ordinary about his beloved. In fact, he assures her that he sees her as a beautiful flower among thorns.

The bride speaks again in verse 3: *"As the apple tree among the trees of the wood, so is my beloved among the sons. I sat down under his shadow with great delight, and his fruit was sweet to my taste."* The bride also looks through special eyes and she assures her beloved that among the many trees of the forest, he is like a refreshing, delightful apple tree. No one else blesses her life; no other refreshes and sustains her. Only her beloved fulfills these roles.

This kind of special look sees beyond the years of aging and beholds the beautiful person your mate is becoming. Gentleness and carefulness in expressing the joy you feel at the beauty of your wife or the delightfulness of your husband make closeness possible.

Lives in a *special security* 2:8-14

From earlier sessions, you will recall that this text is the practical demonstration of *storge* love. While the word itself is not in the Bible, the manifestation and definition is certainly expressed. This comfortable security of fitting together, belonging to each other, and fully trusting each other is clearly seen in this passage and in two verses in particular.

Note that the manifestation of this special kind of security is expressed in verse 9. "*My beloved is like a roe or a young hart: behold, he standeth behind our wall, he looketh forth at the windows, shewing himself through the lattice.*" As we observed in previous sessions, lingering behind the wall and looking through the lattice would be strictly off-limits to anyone else. This privacy, viewed by any other, would be an invasion. Because the couple has the sense of security and trust, however, this is a place shared together because they belong.

This special kind of security is also declared in verse 14. "*O my dove, that art in the clefts of the rock, in the secret places of the stairs, let me see thy countenance, let me hear thy voice; for sweet is thy voice, and thy countenance is comely.*" Standing in the secret place of the stairs demonstrates the couple living in special security and trust. They live in unique places of intimacy that are strictly off limits to everyone else.

> **Optional Teaching Point—Pause the DVD.**
> Take a few moments to explore with your couples those things that build security. Ask the couples to share several "marriage security-builders." These may include such answers as time shared together, expressing affirmation and appreciation, encouraging each other, and being affectionate. Then take a few moments and encourage the couples to share things that tend to damage or destroy security. These may include answers such as taking each other for granted, running each other down, flirting with others, comparing others in a positive way to the mate, making threatening statements, and being harsh with each other. These are reminders of previously mentioned details. This is meant to reinforce the importance of their application.
> **After the discussion, resume the DVD.**

See the significance of the statement of closeness in the words, "My beloved is mine, and I am his…" This pledging of your life to your mate is the giving of yourself unconditionally so long as life shall last.

Learns in a *special relationship* 2:16

See the significance of the statement of closeness in the words, "*My beloved is mine, and I am his….*" This pledging of your life to your mate is the giving of yourself unconditionally so long as life shall last. As this commitment continues through the years, there will be many opportunities to learn, grow, and be stretched in your relationship.

Although you will not use the wording that Solomon and his beloved used, successful marriages that build closeness will employ these same principles. Be sure that your mate knows how special he or she really is to you.

> **Optional Conclusion—You may stop the DVD here.**
>
> Wise couples understand that marriages either grow closer and deeper in connection by building bridges or they will slowly drift apart because of carelessness or thoughtlessness.
>
> Use the illustration of the lawn and bank account to close this session. Making arrangements ahead of time to have a couple briefly share their testimony would be a great way to conclude this session.
>
> This week, take seriously the great opportunity of demonstrating your desire for closeness to your mate.
>
> ***
>
> If you chose the **Optional conclusion** then begin the next viewing of the DVD "What Makes Closeness Possible" with the following material:
>
> - Review the marriage of Timothy and Elizabeth.
> - Remind the couples that the Lord makes closeness throughout their marriage possible.
> - Rehearse with the couples the principles of looking through special eyes, living in special security, and learning in a special relationship.
>
> **Open with prayer and begin the DVD.**

The FACTS

Here are five very special things learned from actual couples who live throughout the United States that you can do to build closeness in your marriage. By employing the word "*FACTS*," learn and apply these principles to develop the closeness the Lord desires for your marriage.

(Extra space will be provided for additional notes from the DVD.)

> **Just the FACTS:**
> **F**reely give self to mate.
> **A**ppreciate God's design & **a**ccept His help.
> **C**ast cares upon the Lord.
> **T**rust each other biblically.
> **S**erve the Lord joyfully.

F stands for **Freely gives self to mate**.

Ephesians 5:33; Malachi 2:14; Genesis 2:24, 4:1

Think of the incredible blessing of loving your mate as Christ loves you. Sadly, some couples live in a way that takes and never gives. What wonderful joy comes in living for your mate and giving yourself totally to your partner.

_____

_____

_____

A stands for **Appreciates God's design and accepts His help in building marriage**.

Proverbs 3:5-6, 5:15-20

Marriage is God's idea, and He has a plan for your marriage. You express your appreciation for His design in trusting Him fully and acknowledging or seeking Him always. Accepting His help is not only wise, it is the only way to genuinely grow closer in the way He desires.

C stands for **Casts cares upon the Lord** 1 Peter 5:7.

Trouble will surely come. Disappointments are bound to happen. Plans and dreams are sometimes shattered. Life down here on earth is very hard at times. These difficulties can either push you apart or draw you and your mate together. When hardships come, don't retreat from each other, and don't become bitter with the Lord. Intentionally reach out to each other and together cast your care upon the Lord. Talk with the Lord and describe your heartache. Then tell Him you are giving it to Him. Picture leaving your heartache with the Lord. Don't be surprised if you must do this more than just once!

_____

_____

_____

_____

_____

_____

_____

T stands for <u>**Treats each other biblically**</u> **Matthew 7:12.**

Some call this the royal or golden rule. Actually, it is the blessed rule that reminds you to treat others the way you wish to be treated. Think of this in a very practical way by answering these questions:

How would you like to be respected?

How would you like to be appreciated?

How would you like to be complimented?

How would you like to be encouraged?

How would you like to be loved and cherished?

Make these responses the way you treat your mate.

_____

_____

_____

_____

_____

_____

_____

S stands for <u>**Serves the Lord joyfully**</u> **Psalm 100:2; Matthew 22:37.**

Couples who joyfully serve the Lord together often find that their love and connection really grows. How wonderful it is to be committed to serving the Lord because both husband and wife love Him.

_____

_____

_____

Closing reading

> Since the Lord Jesus said in John 13:17,
> "If ye know these things, happy are ye if ye do them,"
>
> I surely know the assignment before me
> is to cooperate with the Lord
> in building closeness in my marriage.
>
> It is not so much that I want to change my mate,
> as I want the Lord to change me.
>
> Well, maybe I really do want to change my mate,
> But deep down in my heart,
> I know the Lord needs to change me.
>
> So beginning today, I want to genuinely live for the Lord Jesus.
> I want to overcome the barriers.
> I want to build bridges.
> I want to guard against taking my mate for granted.
> I want to make each day count for the Lord and my mate.
>
> And Lord, You know
> it will be a whole lot more pleasant and workable,
> if You would so move in my mate's heart,
> to want these same things.
>
> Closeness to You, and to my mate, is my desire.
>
> May our connection be real and our devotion obvious, dear Lord.

DVD concludes

Make the most of the moment

> *Encourage them to take a serious inventory of their marriage. Tenderly lead them to make a serious commitment to connect with each other and build closeness on the journey of a lifetime.*

Your couples have been challenged, and encouraged, by the statements of other couples across America. The FACTS of successful marriage building and connection are personal, powerful, and practical. Take a moment to review these principles with your couples. Encourage them to take a serious inventory of their marriage. Tenderly lead them to make a serious commitment to connect with each other and build closeness on the journey of a lifetime.

Let's work on connecting this week

Think of the younger Timothy and Elizabeth who asked the elderly Timothy and Elizabeth for counsel and suggestions in building their marriage.

❶ List five things you believe are essential in building successful marriages.

_____

_____

_____

_____

_____

_____

_____

❷ This week, make a date with each other to go to a private place where you can really talk. Ideally, get out of town, secure a room in a nice hotel, make it an overnight together to talk about your marriage, each other, and what the Lord desires for you.

Do not take the entire time just talking. Do things together and, by all means, have fun together on this adventure! Make your marriage the highlight, and take time to really talk with each other and pray for one another and your marriage.

If an overnight is not possible, still create a getaway atmosphere by going to a local park to talk about your relationship. Share your dreams and goals. Talk about your relationship with the Lord, and list some of His many blessings with each other.

In your conversation, talk about your answers to the following questions.
— What place does the Lord hold in our marriage and home?
— How do we view each other? What do we really mean to each other, and how do we express this?
— Do we really understand the difference between a covenant and a contract?
— How can we better express the concept of cherishing each other?
— Can we identify any wall that exists between us? If so, do we know how to remove it? Would we be willing to get help with this situation?

— In the expression of our love, how are we doing in the friendship, romance, security, passion, and unconditional commitment aspects?
— Understanding that genuine love must be demonstrated, what means the most to each of you from the following list?
  - The touches of endearment
  - The words of value and worth
  - The little things I give or make
  - The actions of thoughtfulness
  - The moments we share together
  - The specific things we do to bless each other
  - The memories we make together
  - The reminders of our love
— How can we better demonstrate these to each other?
— Would we as a couple be willing to make a note of the acrostic WAFFLE and deliberately choose to implement these characteristics daily?
— Are we ready to commit to daily reading God's Word and praying together?

❸ Write out a testimony of what the Lord is doing in your marriage. Try to put it into words as a matter of praise to the Lord for His blessings and what He is teaching you.

_____
_____
_____
_____
_____
_____
_____
_____

> Encourage them to take a serious inventory of their marriage. Tenderly lead them to make a serious commitment to connect with each other and build closeness on the journey of a lifetime.

Would you be willing to share this as a couple in a church service or as a way to promote this DVD for the next set of couples to view it?

Additional things the Lord is teaching me

_____
_____
_____

Chapter 6—The Leader's Friend

Additional Aids & Special Counseling Helps

"The greatest help that you render to others is sharing God's Word, and living the life before others that you are encouraging them to live. A great teacher is first a precious example."

"But thou hast fully known my doctrine, manner of life, purpose, faith, longsuffering, charity, patience."
(2 Timothy 3:10)

As you work with the couples God has entrusted to you, you will occasionally encounter couples who require further assistance and counsel. You may copy and distribute these aids in your ministry. Should you desire to change any of the aids, please contact Dr. Michael Peck at Baptist Church Planters (440-748-1677) for permission.

Daily Bible Reading Plan

For those couples who never established the priority of having a devotional time together, you can suggest the following 50-day Bible reading plan. The couple should be looking for ways the Lord Jesus is revealed and glorified. Also, take a few minutes to discuss how each day's passage applies to their daily lives and marriage.

This Bible reading takes the couples through the Gospel of John in 50 days. Christ is presented as God the Son. He is worthy of our worship, and obedience.

> For those couples who never established the priority of having a devotional time together, you can suggest the following 50-day Bible reading plan.

Day	Scripture Reading	Day	Scripture Reading
1	John 1:1-18	26	John 11:1-27
2	John 1:19-34	27	John 11:28-44
3	John 1:35-51	28	John 11:45-57
4	John 2:1-11	29	John 12:1-11
5	John 2:12-25	30	John 12:12-19
6	John 3:1-21	31	John 12:20-36
7	John 3:22-36	32	John 12:37-50
8	John 4:1-27	33	John 13:1-20
9	John 4:28-54	34	John 13:21-38
10	John 5:1-18	35	John 14:1-14
11	John 5:19-32	36	John 14:15-26
12	John 5:33-47	37	John 14:27-31
13	John 6:1-21	38	John 15:1-27
14	John 6:22-40	39	John 16:1-15
15	John 6:41-71	40	John 16:16-33
16	John 7:1-29	41	John 17:1-26
17	John 7:30-53	42	John 18:1-23
18	John 8:1-11	43	John 18:24-40
19	John 8:12-30	44	John 19:1-24
20	John 8:31-59	45	John 19:25-42
21	John 9:1-12	46	John 20:1-18
22	John 9:13-41	47	John 20:19-25
23	John 10:1-18	48	John 20:26-31
24	John 10:19-30	49	John 21:1-14
25	John 10:31-42	50	John 21:15-25

15 Ways to Build a Strong Marriage

In some ways, marriages are similar to building a house. Both must be built on strong foundations, directions must be followed, and careful attention must be given to details. Developing a daily consistency in the following areas will help you to build a strong marriage. It is well worth the time and investment.

1. Be sure that you and your mate are becoming best friends.
2. Develop good conversational skills. Do not interrupt. Look at each other. Speak clearly without sarcasm or hurtful words.
3. Share openly with each other about your fears, concerns, and thoughts.
4. Learn to be considerate of your mate's feelings.
5. Develop the skill to become better aware of the little details of life and the home, which will demonstrate thoughtfulness to your mate.
6. Avoid developing a critical spirit. Do not criticize your mate. When you must address a situation, express it carefully, prayerfully, and tenderly.
7. Frequently tell your mate of your love.
8. Become good in demonstrating that you are not taking your mate for granted.
9. Never be in competition with your mate.
10. Discover God's purpose for your life.
11. Determine to grow as a Christian.
12. Find ways to serve the Lord together.
13. Ask the Lord to help you to reach an agreement concerning earning, savings, investing, spending, and sharing your money.
14. Respect your mate.
15. Work at having a great relationship with the extended family. Always remember, however, that your first priority is the Lord and the next is your mate.

The Top 10 Wise Things That Smart Couples Still Do

Great marriages do not just happen. Saying "I do" on your wedding day with little or no investment and involvement in your marriage is not a guarantee of a happy and growing relationship. Those couples who stay happily married for decades all seem to have a common thread interwoven throughout their marriage. In addition to trusting the Lord Jesus for salvation, these couples identify and consistently implement 10 important things in their lives:

10. *Talk to each other graciously*—Proverbs 10:11, 19-20, 32.
9. *Seek God's will earnestly*—Psalm 143:10. There is no greater joy than doing the plan that God shows a couple, in the place God leads the couple, with the people God entrusts to the couple, through the power the Lord gives to the couple.
8. *Treat each other thoughtfully*—Matthew 19:5-6. The tender and thoughtful courtesies extended to each other throughout the dating process

> Great marriages do not just happen. Couples who stay happily married for decades all seem to have a common thread interwoven throughout their marriage. In addition to trusting the Lord Jesus for salvation, these couples identify and consistently implement 10 important things in their lives.

continue on and grow far beyond the marriage ceremony. Every day provides new opportunities to demonstrate consideration and kindness to each other. A thoughtful action greatly assists the one-flesh unity of which the Lord speaks. Unkind and thoughtless acts push couples apart and hurt the one-flesh unity.

7. *Forgive those hurts quickly*—Ephesians 4:30-32. No marriage is perfect. Every couple has plenty of opportunities to give and receive forgiveness.

6. *Cast their cares on the Lord completely*—1 Peter 5:7. Throughout the lifetime of marriage, every couple will endure a wide variety of experiences. Some of the greatest joys and blessings will come as will some of the greatest heartaches and disappointments. In the hard times, the couple's marriage will be blessed as they quietly and deliberately cast their cares upon the Lord.

   Couples who pray together, embrace each other, and cherish each other in the hard times will find a great source of strength in the trial as they apply this great Bible principle.

5. *Model their roles biblically*—Ephesians 5:21-33. What a vivid object lesson the Lord displays in the lives of the husband and wife! The role of the husband is to biblically model the life of love, devotion, and commitment of Christ to the Church. Holding nothing back that is helpful, the devoted husband lives for his wife and gives her a cherished place held by no other person.

   Likewise, the love, devotion, and respect that the Church renders to the Lord is modeled in a beautiful way in the life of the godly wife. The submission spoken of in the text is not that of fear and burden. It is the respect and loyalty of a godly wife who looks to her husband for leadership, protection, and wisdom.

4. *View their children thankfully*—Psalm 127-128. In the timing and plan of the Lord, children are a wonderful blessing. While sometimes a great challenge, children are ultimately a joy. Wise couples often tell their children how thankful they are that God has brought them into their lives.

3. *Affirm their devotion tenderly*—Proverbs 5:15-20. The writer of Proverbs is very frank and forthcoming about the joy of one husband and one wife finding sexual thrill and satisfaction exclusively within their marriage relationship. Wise couples affirm their devotion consistently.

2. *Serve the Lord together gladly*—Psalm 100:2. Wise couples are not only members of the local church, they are faithful and active and find opportunities to serve the Lord.

1. *Love each other totally*—Song of Solomon 2:16. They belong to each other. This is the *agape* love that is a decision of the will, seeking the

well-being and best interests of the other, even when it is not deserved. Such love holds back anything that is hurtful, rude, arrogant or self-serving. The wise couple, knowing their marriage is for a lifetime, daily seeks opportunity not only to love each other but to discover ways to express it to each other. Instead of the words "me" and "I," the common expression becomes "we" and "us."

Be an Example of a Great Marriage

"Be ye followers of me, even as I also am of Christ" (1 Corinthians 11:1). What a powerful statement the Apostle Paul made! Without boasting or bragging, Paul gently told the Corinthian believers that they could follow him as he was following Christ. This is the exact principle that your own marriage, as a spiritual leader, should reflect. As you and your mate follow the Lord, others should be able to pattern their marriage after yours.

This is challenging and sobering. Begin today to really build your own marriage. Embrace the qualifications of 1 Timothy 3:1-7, even if you are not a pastor. Building a great marriage is a great blessing. Think of a few of the blessings.

> Begin today to really build your own marriage. Embrace the qualifications of 1 Timothy 3:1-7, even if you are not a pastor. Building a great marriage is a great blessing.

1. *A great friendship*—Song of Solomon 2:4, "...His banner over me is love." The bride of Solomon was delighted that the love of her life was also her very best friend.

2. *A great example*—1 Corinthians 11:1, "Be ye followers of me, even as I also am of Christ," is not the statement of arrogance. It is rather the honest, quiet expression of surrender to the Lord and consistent living of His principles. Though the couple may not say it in words, others will be able to see the results of a great marriage and say, "I want my marriage to be like theirs."

3. *A great prayer support*—1 Peter 3:7. A dishonored marriage relationship results in a hindered prayer life. What an incredible connection takes place when the husband and wife are prayer partners! What a wonderful blessing in the life of a great marriage!

4. *A great opportunity to demonstrate a servant's spirit*—Romans 6:22. Writing to the church at Rome, Paul reminded these early believers that they were freed from being slaves to sin. Now they would discover the joy of being servants of the Lord with fruitful and holy living unto Him. Great marriages are not harsh, demanding, and self-centered. When husband and wife overcome the temptation to be arrogant, thoughtless, and hard to live with, a beautiful desire to live for each other grows into genuine service.

5. *A great illustration is possible*—Ephesians 5:21-33. The illustration of Christ and His church is demonstrated beautifully by a godly husband

and his wife. Love, protection, and devotion evidenced in the life of the husband, as well as respect, submission, and appreciation modeled by the godly wife combine to beautifully illustrate the spiritual reality of Christ and the church.

6. *Great security is enjoyed*—Proverbs 24:3. Trust is a wonderful thing. It takes time to grow and develop. Unfortunately, it can be damaged or ruined very quickly. The security of a marriage and home built on wisdom and understanding results in a security that brings quiet stability and certain trust even in the hardest of times.

7. *Great spotlight for right convictions*—Joshua 24:15. At the conclusion of his public ministry, Joshua with great conviction and determination thundered, "…But as for me and my house, we will serve the Lord." Public ministry and private living combine to spotlight right convictions and a lifestyle that is powerful and believable to others.

8. *Great testimony of faithfulness*—1 Corinthians 4:2. Specifically Paul states that the chief requirement of stewardship is the attribute of faithfulness. In the wise managing and handling of their marriage relationship, the Lord requires the believing couple to be faithful. Remaining faithful to the Lord and to each other results in joy that is hard to express.

9. *Great safeguard*—Ecclesiastes 9:9. A "one husband and one wife, as long as life shall last" kind of joyfulness is a great safeguard against sinfulness and foolishness. The writer of Ecclesiastes reminds his readers that after trying everything imaginable, there is nothing like living joyfully with one's wife all of life. This is great counsel for wise living.

10. *Great partnership*—1 Timothy 3:2. For those in pastoral positions, the phrase "the husband of one wife" is far more than simply making it through a lifetime without divorcing. Rather, the idea literally is expressed in the pastor so loving his wife that he actually becomes a one-woman kind of man.

    Becoming a one-woman kind of man and a one-man kind of woman is a wonderful blessing that results from a great marriage. This kind of partnership requires care and devotion as well as help from the Lord. It is a blessing indeed and one to be sought after with great diligence.

Other Resources by Dr. Michael Peck

From This Day Forward – Preparing Couples for the Journey of a Lifetime. This resource is available in both the Counselor's edition as well as the Couple's edition.

Steps of Joy – Preparing for Membership in My Local Church is available for the adult and student. Ten lessons prepare men and women to become strong and godly members of their local church.

Steps of Joy for Boys and Girls prepares children for local church membership. A special feature of this resource is the S-W-A-P, which means a "story with a purpose." Written from the perspective of the child, biblical principles are clearly identified.

Discovering and Developing Leaders is available in both the instructor and student editions, along with the accompanying DVD. Future leaders must be found and developed in local churches through the Scriptures and a practical plan.

Visit our web site www.bcpusa.org to order materials. Be watching for further resources on marriage and parenting.

www.ingramcontent.com/pod-product-compliance
Lightning Source LLC
Chambersburg PA
CBHW080523110426

42742CB00017B/3213